To Dragoslava, my dear companion whose sacrifice of hard work and dedicated love, during our stay at Yale, highly contributed to writing of this book,

And to every soul in this graceless world who seeks to be embraced by the Other and who desires to embrace the other for the purpose of life worth living . . .

CONTENTS

FOREWORD

SOME WOULD SAY THAT the wounds are still too fresh for a book like this one to be written. Alexander Santrač, the author, is a Serbian philosopher and theologian. I, the person whose theology is the subject of the book, am Croatian. Our two nations have been at war until recently and tensions between many Croats and Serbs still run high. The fuel for both the war and the tensions are mutual recriminations and, interminable incompatible stories of domination and brutal victimization. The conflict left traces both of us. His truth about the common history of our nations looks like a Serbian truth to me, and mine looks like a Croatian truth to him, and our different truths would clash if we would just let them. The sources of our pains are correspondingly different, too. Yet the unlikely book is here.

At one level, *Witness to Life Worth Living* is a critical scholarly engagement with my work—an account of my theology flanked by a brief and fragmentary story of some of the earliest influences on my spiritual and intellectual development as well as by critical evaluations of some positions I take. I am grateful that Alex, as I have come to call him now that we have become friends, has taken the time and effort to study my scholarly publications, listen to many public lectures, read numerous popular interviews I have given, and then synthesize everything into a coherent vision that informs and energizes the entire corpus of my work. Dissertations have been written about aspects of my theology—my theology of work, ecclesiology, aspects of reconciliation, or account of memory—but this is the first book-length treatment of my theology as a whole.

There is another, perhaps more important, level to Alex' book. What is unique and, given our backgrounds, improbable about it is this: He dared to leave the secure ground of scholarly analysis and venture into the choppy waters of lived experience. His venture into personal, social, and public domains fits well, though, with the kind of theology I advocate. As he rightly notes, the entirety of my intellectual endeavors—from explorations of the transcendent nature of inner Trinitarian relations to the contestation of the legitimacy of torture, to name two examples of things about which I have written—is about a way of life; more precisely, it is about varieties of truthful *ways* of living in the Spirit of Jesus Christ, as each one of us will have our own way of "being Christ" and acting like Christ. My theology aims both to persuade the intellect and convert the heart; it seeks to offer truthful critical rendering of a flourishing life marked by love, peace, and joy and to "join God" in generating just such life in persons, communities, and planetary processes. At the most basic level, it is about earthly echoes of God's life and love, faint as these echoes might often be. It is fitting then that an account of my theology would be dotted with the author's own personal stories—a family tragedy, a missionary mishap, an intercultural encounter, and a religious contestation, to name a few. The stories of these tension-filled experiences serve to display what I have called "livability" of theology.

I have been described as "a theologian of the bridge." Alex's book about my theology is an exercise in bridge building. Perhaps his unlikely book was able to be written because at the foundation of what both Alex and I consider to be ultimately true, good, and beautiful is the One whose very being is "bridge:" God, understood not as an utterly singular monad but a Trinitarian field of love, and Christ, that same God having assumed human flesh so as be the bridge on which humanity can walk to redemption. It is in this God that both Alex and I ultimately place our hope that we, the tellers of unending self-exculpatory and other-accusatory stories that keep feeding on mutually reinforcing cycles of deception, injustice, and violence, might find our way to God and to each other. This kind of bridge building is just what theology is for.

Miroslav Volf

PREFACE

MIROSLAV VOLF OPENS HIS most influential book, *Exclusion and Embrace*, with the question, "Can you embrace a *chetnik*?"[1] Volf, a Croat, writing in the mid-1990s when the Croats and Serbs were engaged in a bitter war, was referring to *chetnik* (the representative of the radical Serbian military movement with an original purpose of defense of the Serbian royal family and the Yugoslavian first resistance movement, later involved in establishment of an ethnically "pure" Serbian land).[2] A similar question had lingered in my own mind for a long time before it materialized again on that early September night in 1992: "Can I really embrace *Ustasha*?" I am a Serb, and *Ustasha* is the representative of the Croatian regime that slaughtered tens if not hundreds of thousands of innocent civilians—Serbs, Gypsies and Jews, with their children—in Jasenovac concentration camp, one of the most criminal WWII camps of the pro-Nazi Croatian puppet government from 1941 to 1945.[3]

It happened a few days after my 20th birthday. I was at the Yugoslavian military base on the Prevlaka peninsula, Montenegro's disputed piece of coast at the border with Croatia, with a critical strategic significance at the entrance to Boka Kotorska Bay. I was in the trench dug that same night, holding my firearm tightly and waiting on the "enemy" from the sea, surrounded by fellow soldiers who all belonged to the same Yugoslavian army

---

1 Volf, *Exclusion and Embrace*, 9.

2 See Milazzo, *Chetnik Movement and the Yugoslavian Resistance.*

3 Ustasha has become a cultural symbol of "mass murder" (see Yeomans, *Visions of Annihilation*, 2). Yeomans believes that half a million people perished during this period. For research on Jasenovac concentration camp atrocities see Lituchy, *Jasenovac and the Holocaust in Yugoslavia.*

—Slovenians, Croats, Bosnians, Macedonians, and my fellow Serbs. There was a full moon, and the night was oddly peaceful. We could hear the howling of Prevlaka's coyotes in the distance, thoroughly bewildered and terrified of what was to come. The previous evening Captain B. had announced that we would be under attack by the Croat army from the Adriatic coast and that the moment had come to defend the fatherland. I was sure that all of us, 20-year-old confused fellows in our Yugoslavian Army, asked ourselves the same pounding question: "What is my fatherland now?" Of course, all of us were intensely looking at the Croat soldiers that were part of our own army. They stayed calm, but the distant look in their eyes revealed suppressed fear of the unknown. It was a tension-filled night for all of us. I was looking in the direction of one of my Croat fellow-soldiers, who unfortunately a few days before had stolen all my favorite music CDs. These CDs were my only comfort during the long and lonesome nights in the radar. Nevertheless, later on I was glad that I was robbed, since that music had become incompatible with my Christian identity and the sense of divine presence. I had seen the CDs in his private soldier box but I said nothing, since as a new soldier I was fearful of reprisals.

At that precise moment, I could have used the opportunity to harm him, since all Croat soldiers in our army had suddenly become mortal enemies overnight. Nevertheless, even though I desperately wished for some form of revenge, I realized I would not be able to retaliate, since I was constantly "praying" to the unknown God (for the first time in my life) not to commit murder. This prayer had become a desperate attempt to connect myself with some type of metaphysical or transcendent reality in the midst of ethical dilemma. Spiritual loneliness was unbearable. All of us were ready for the attackers and I was gripped by my inner conflict and wondering how it might be resolved. It was not possible to bypass this unpleasantness and a palpable sense of loss.

Fortunately, my conscience worked properly and I was surprised by that miraculous fact. This religious experience was transformed into a sacred, mystical encounter with the Unknown Other emptied of both cataphatic and apophatic theology,[4] pressing my *sensus moralis* to do the right thing. I felt the wonder and astonishment of the unexpected. It would be very difficult to identify, analyze, describe or explain either the cause or the effect of this phenomenal experience. Nonetheless, it certainly happened as

---

4 These are technical terms for positive or negative claims about God based on the assumption of God-language limitations (See Taliaferro, *Philosophy of Religion,* 25).

a result of my striving for freedom from the unbearable tension of an ethical dilemma. "Ask and it will be given to you; seek and you will find; knock and the door will be opened to you."[5] Seeking was clumsy, yet rewarding.

Suddenly, there in those trenches, one of the officers arrived and invited all Croat soldiers to turn in all their weapons and equipment. Sighs of relief issued from all of us, including them. At least their lives would be spared that night. All of them were escorted to the nearby military prison and they stayed there until further notice. Of course, the soldier who had stolen my CDs was in that group. I never visited him (no one did) and shortly all of them were transferred to another prison and were eventually released to go home and participate in another war for Croatian independence.

Luckily, there was no direct conflict that night and I was praising Providence for hearing the prayer of a sinner. Though, according to Hume's reflection on miracles, "wise man proportions his belief to the evidence"[6] or *probability* of events, I had a reason/evidence to believe in a high probability of unusual events in my life, namely, miracles. The ultimate Providence was transformed into the ultimate Grace that penetrates the hardest of hearts. I was thrilled by the fact that there was no need to harm anyone. Later on, the Yugoslavian army selected some other more experienced groups and veterans to go and fight on the front line. Newcomers were spared. Working on the radar system in the noncombatant workforce, I was grateful to be among these young recruits. I spent an additional peaceful year on Prevlaka reading and absorbing every bit of Christian wisdom from the Scriptures and Christian tradition. Providentially, what looked like becoming my life's failure or even a termination has become the greatest triumph! In fact, the war crisis helped me to find the face of the Unknown Other, the face of Christ, the Crucified and Resurrected One, who eventually revealed himself to me as the ultimate Grace by *embracing* me, the sinner, and by transforming me to *embrace* the other.

Regretfully, however, that night of my first childish, desperate prayer for safety, in my mind the unknown Croat soldier still was transformed into an *ustasha*. He had become the perpetrator, the symbol of the most distant otherness, a metaphor of an exclusion by necessity and historical inertia. That arduous night I remembered vividly, though perhaps wrongly, how

5. Matt 7:7 (NIV).

6 D. Hume, "Enquiry Concerning Human Understanding," quoted in Taliaferro, *Philosophy of Religion*, 134.

my family name Santrac was one of the prominent Serbian last names on the endless list of people executed in Jasenovac, the Auschwitz of the Balkans. I remembered, too, how some of my Serbian friends from Croatia never had any difficulties before revealing that they were ethnic Serbs. Nevertheless, I did not want to terminate somebody's life, even on the basis of justified revenge, or of retributive justice, or of the "sacred identity" of my ethnicity. Perhaps the miraculous prayer indeed awakened the need for restorative justice. The Croat soldier was a thief, but for me he was much more than a robber: he had become the incarnation of, and the metaphor for, all past evils done to my family name, the Serbian people and my homeland. Yet, in spite of these wrongful memories, I could not have harmed anyone. I did feel compassion for the soldier and I still was not a converted fully-fledged Christian. I even managed to smile, not cynically. Healing has commenced.

Was that a first step towards the reality of *embrace* triggered by the proper function of my *sensus divinitatus*?[7] Was the scandal of hatred and exclusion gradually transforming into exhilarating hope for universal love and embrace? I am not sure if I was ready then to open my arms, and I am not sure how my phenomenology of embrace[8] worked, but if my friend had opened his arms I would certainly have embraced him, not because I respected him or affectionately loved him, but because Providence that night expanded my space by mysterious grace alone. I even pondered the existential idea of Volf's "double vision," for making an effort to be "there" in my Croat fellow-soldier's reality changed my perspective on being "here."[9] Imagining him in prison or going to another war at home, I even started contemplating his anguishes. Empathy for him and his compatriots was prompted by the unknown transcendent stimulus working on my sense of divinity. Meaninglessness of war made me claustrophobic and nauseous in the trenches. One thing was certain: I was not apathetic. My experience back there was indeed enigmatic and unfathomable! It defied logic and structure.

I was never taught to hate Croats, Albanians, Muslims, or any other ethnic group. On the contrary, I marched proudly as one of Tito's "pioneers" with the blue cap and a red star, white shirt and red tie. "Brotherhood and unity" was the prevailing political, social and, "spiritual" slogan

---

7. See my *Comparison of John Calvin and Alvin Plantinga's Concept of Sensus Divinitatis.*

8. Volf, *Exclusion and Embrace,* 140.

9. Ibid., 250-53.

of ex-Yugoslavia, and it did benefit us all. My father was a son of a communist Serb from Bosnia who immigrated to Vojvodina (northern Serbia) in 1948, and my mother's parents belonged to the heart of the 1941 Serbian Partisan (communist) resistance movement in their teenage years. Nonetheless, when I joined the army in 1991 as a nineteen-year-old fellow (military service was compulsory) I came to realize and learn that so-called friends, comrades and brothers were mortal enemies and that *exclusion* was preferable to *embrace*. Through historical inertia and moral indolence the necessity for exclusion pervaded all our social interaction and ethnic identity. Boundaries have never become permeable!

By the time of the NATO bombing of Serbia (operation "Merciful Angel" in 1999), an event that was welcomed and praised by some of my Croat "Christian" friends, I realized I did not really like their proximity and company in spite of the fact that by that time I had become a mature Christian, or at least I thought so. How could they welcome "Merciful Angel" when this "angel" was destroying my people's innocent children and civilians? Though I clearly understood NATO's justification for this operation, militaristic imperialism or collateral damage simply were not part of my moral dictionary. During that NATO campaign I studied in the USA towards my Master's degree in religion. My mother phoned and informed me that I was drafted several times to the Serbian army, and again I was praising graciousness of God for possibly sparing my life. Radars were the primary targets of NATO missiles. Again I had no intention of taking *anyone's* life. My commitment to anti-militarism and pacifism became even stronger. The public media, saturated with images from war-ravaged areas, forced us to stay within our camps, suspiciously pointing fingers at enemies who wanted to destroy our land and our sacred identity. This time the Albanians had become the villains, and the Kosovo War had become utterly dirty. Though I strongly believed in a historical and spiritual sense of sacredness of the Serbian lands and identity in Kosovo[10] (and I still do), as a follower of the Crucified One I had to step back from nationalism and emotional involvement. My endurance almost came to an end. Frustration piled up. Again, the steps towards

10. Kosovo, an impoverished land with a mainly Albanian population, unilaterally declared independence from Serbia in February 2008, after years of strained relations between its Serb and Albanian inhabitants (BBC's Kosovo Profile, Nov. 11, 2014). Nonetheless, the sacredness of Kosovo land will always remain in the heart of every Serb since it represents the historical myth of Serbian identity. The defeat of Serbia by the Ottoman Empire in 1389 became, in the long run, the triumph of the Cross. Moreover, the seat of the Serbian Orthodox Church was at Kosovo for a long time.

the embrace of the other (enemy) were deemed impossible and undesirable. Moreover, indifference lurked as a final cynical response to the unbearable pain of exclusion. Unresponsiveness seemed like a viable option for a Christian like me. But the Providence had a plan.

ACKNOWLEDGMENTS

FIRST OF ALL, I would like to express my deepest appreciation to Miroslav Volf, Henry B. Wright Professor of Systematic Theology, Founding Director of the Yale Center for Faith & Culture, and my faculty sponsor at Yale Divinity School for his extraordinary generosity and cordiality, contribution in stimulating interviews, extremely valuable comments after reading the first manuscript of this work, and for time and efforts devoted to writing of a foreword. Without his crucial role in the mutually enriching dialogue with me this work would not be possible. Miroslav indeed demonstrated the true spirit of friendliness and Christian charity.

I express my gratitude to Dr Stuart Rochester for the editing/formatting of this work and *finalizing this project within the limited time frame,* and Brian Palmer and Matthew Wimer from Wipf and Stock for the publication of this book.

Furthermore, I would like to thank in a special way Dr Cheryl Kisunzu, the Provost of Washington Adventist University, MD and Dr Patrick Williams, the Associate Provost and Dean of the School of Arts and Sciences, for their visionary leadership, academic friendship, encouragement and recognition of the value of this book as well as financial support for editing of the work.

Finally, my wife Dragoslava and my two daughters Nastasja Nadia and Emily Grace deserve special appreciation for their understanding of this golden opportunity to do one of the most important projects in my life.

INTRODUCTION

FINALLY, IN 2014, HERE I am at Yale Divinity School, as a visiting fellow in Christian Ethics, venturing to explore the meaning of an *ethics of embrace* and of *life worth living*. I was brought here by the same Providence that taught me not to retaliate or harm another human being and empowered my sense of divinity to take a first step towards the pacifistic embrace. My faculty sponsor, Miroslav Volf, the Croat, one of the most notable evangelical, Episcopalian, and ecumenical theologians of our time, might possibly, I thought, be ready to open his arms to embrace me, the Serb, the "*chetnik*" from the Yugoslavian/Serbian army who destroyed his fatherland.[1] Would he see in me one of the members of the *Tigers* (members of the Serbian Volunteer Guard who, partially supported by the Serbian government at the time, spread dread and fear among the Croat and Muslim military and civilian population in the 1990s and beyond)? Or, more currently speaking, a member of the Serbian Radical (Nationalistic) Party, which desperately tries to break ties with the West and find shelter under the wings of "mother" Russia? If this might be an exaggeration, perhaps I might become a certain potent metaphor of otherness and ultimate distance for him in the same way as the unknown Croat soldier had become a symbol of exclusion for me? This embrace may become clumsy and risky.

Though Volf rightly mentioned to me that "we commit injustice and sin against love when a concrete individual serves as a metaphor of (perceived) exclusion perpetrated by the group to which he or she belongs, and that in itself is a form of exclusion,"[2] I cannot resist the temptation of putting the embrace/exclusion theology into the concrete context of our growing

1. Volf, *Exclusion and Embrace*, 9.
2. Volf, to author, May 2015.

relationship. In spite of our clear identities as disciples of the Crucified and Resurrected One, the fabric of our selves is saturated with historical memories of animosities. I therefore ask myself a few important questions. Would I be ready to embrace Professor Volf in return? What could I see in him? The Serbian national anthem starts with the words "Bože pravde"—the God of Justice. If I were to pursue the path of retributive justice (an improper, even wrongful, function of my spiritual sense) I might see in him an executioner in Jasenovac, or, in more contemporary terms, Alojzije Stepinac (the Croatian Cardinal who contributed to the forceful conversion of Serbs and who is currently on the list for sainthood). For some, Stepinac was a "cardinal of genocide," for others a "martyr of communism." Or would Volf maybe betray his "ethics of embrace" by a cynical smile over the success of NATO bombings, or the joy of victory in the "Oluja" (Storm) or "Bljesak" (Lightning) operations (the expulsion of hundreds of thousands of Serb civilians from their native land Croatia by the Croatian government and military, supported by the West in 2005)?

Why have I come to Yale after all? We cannot even play the same game—Miroslav plays soccer and I play basketball! He has two sons, and I have two daughters. In our potential dialogue the rules seem very different. The distance seems to be unbridgeable. Will we be engaged in disputes about how the past events should be remembered? How can we find the common "language game"[3] that leads to ultimate embrace and common good and love? I know that both of us, as disciples of Christ, should be looking ahead, but the past always lurks as a serpent ready to infuse the poison of exclusion and remoteness, especially if we succumb again to the twenty-first century ambiguous contemporary sentiments of our fellow citizens. Hope lies only in our persistent Christian commitment to embrace!

As I am writing these words (May 21, 2014) images of devastating floods in the Balkans (Bosnia, Serbia, and parts of Croatia) are tearing my heart apart. People are displaced, drowned, homeless, frightened, and hopeless. Nevertheless, the nostalgic idea of unity in crisis and the brotherhood of these "Yugoslavian" peoples is re-emerging in the media as a potential candidate for a new fresh start full of hope, a renewed "language game" from the past. Even the Serbian tennis player Novak Djokovic, No. 1 in the world, propagates the idea. Unfortunately, renewed militaristic agendas of both East and West, weaponizing small Balkan states, make this project

---

3. Ludwig Wittgenstein's philosophical term used for the contextual understanding of language and the form of living. See Santrac, "Untying the Knots of Thinking."

less and less likely. Had I not believed that there might be hope for a unified "language game" I might not have considered Yale Divinity School.
Volf's and my common Christian identity should be pointing not only to
the re-emergence of the "Yugoslavian" spirit, which is a spirit of this world,
but to *Christ*. It is true that there is a long way between Christ *believed*
or confessed and Christ *lived*. I confidently believe that Volf's work and
personality may become formative even for me, that "his way may become
a way of being somebody—being a bow for the flight of others"[4] including
me, the Serb.

Flying with the historic wings of "Yugoslavian" nostalgic brotherhood seems good, but soaring with the wings of the Christ-centered and
Christ-flavored spirit of fraternity and unity seems better. Yet there is no
unlimited future with such a blemished past. Willingness to embrace only
will not erase violent forms of past exclusions. For this reason it seems that
only Christ-centered memories and Christ-flavored common dreams and
projections might create a space for embrace. I have become thrilled by
the fact that both Volf and I, by the same Providence, were committed and
prepared to explore this space.

After all, what is this paradigm of "ethics of embrace"[5] about? Does
it only superficially soothe our wounded conscience or really provide the
true remedy for all our broken relationships and promises of flourishing
life that is worth living? How feasible is Volf's unique ethical system in the
twenty-first century? How efficient is it in this post-9/11 world in which we
are stunned by a new polarization between East and West, clashes between
civilizations of Islam and Christianity, or the troubling context of renewed
conflict in Ukraine and Syria and the apparent reemergence of the Cold
War? How promising is this paradigmatic ethics for individuals, religions
and peoples/nations? In what ways can it emerge from within the walls of
Christian churches or Christian academic halls like Yale Divinity School?
How can it become the hypothetical ethical framework for engagement in
public faith and the search for flourishing and life worth living?

I have arrived at Yale to read Volf in my own way, hopefully unbiased.
I would like to examine his ethical stance from all possible perspectives—
philosophical, theological, and experiential/poetical, including my own,
autobiographical. My interpretation of Volf's standpoint will be presented

---

4 Volf, *Against the Tide*, 211. Volf writes here about the life and death of a friend,
in fact a Serb.

5 Paradigm based on most general approach to Volf's work.

in three parts that I hope will be truthful to his original intent. First, the ideological/theological background of his ethics of embrace will be explored. On what grounds has Volf developed his ethics of exclusion as a necessary precondition for the need of embrace? Second, the 'ethics of embrace' paradigm with all its phenomenology will be presented and evaluated. Finally, I wish to consider how feasible this ethics is in the contemporary divided and alienated world. What is the potential of this unique approach to reconciliation for becoming the theoretical framework of practical realization in the form of public testimony to faith and the promotion of life worth living? Therefore, I express my thoughts and reflections in this work as ethics of exclusion, ethics of embrace and ethics of public faith. Concerning the methodology of this research, instead of a traditional systematic approach to theories, models and concepts of primary literature, I will blend interpretation of Volf's ethical system and theology of life worth living with my ethical/theological insights and personal encounters with transcendent reality. This might resemble Volf's way of writing after all. Autobiographical notes in this work may strengthen legitimacy and efficacy of both Volf's paradigms: ethics of embrace and life worth living. Finally, this work may become the first comprehensive, certainly not exhaustive, analysis of Volf's thought, and eventually play the role of secondary literature.

One more question before investigation of Volf's ethical conceptions: why ethics and not theology of exclusion and embrace?[6] There is, of course, an assumption that when one deals with ideas of a theoretical theologian the product must become a theological paradigm. This is unavoidable. Yet, I wish to present Volf's system of thought in ethical and not purely theological terms. Volf himself testifies in *Captive to the Word of God* (2010):

> At the heart of every theology lies not simply a plausible intellectual vision but more importantly a compelling account of a way of life, and *that theology is therefore best done from within the pursuit of this way of life.*[7]

Determined to support this brilliant remark that theology is not just an intellectual construct but the reflection of a way of life well grasped from within that life (lived experience of the "language game"), I decided to look at Volf's ideas through the lenses of *ethical* demeanor and my own lived *experience*, assuming that Volf himself pursues that same way of life. In this

---

6. Volf considers that the disciplines of moral theology and ethics are inseparable.

7. Italics added for emphasis. Volf, *Captive to the Word of God*, 43.

way Volf's theology as a "science" provides the important ethical framework for its successful implementation in the life worth living. In the opening lecture of his Systematic Theology class at Yale Divinity School he confirms that the purpose of theology is not abstract doctrinal reasoning but *pursuit of life worth living.*[8] A descriptive account of reality means nothing without our pursuit of the right way of living, concludes Volf. This anthropological pursuit, furthermore, ends up in loving God and loving *neighbor*—both rooted in Christ's unconditional love of humanity. The social ethics of embrace is the manifestation of the right way of living. After all, social ethics, Christian or not, speaks about certain paradigms of interaction between morality and social issues, and Volf, as a defining voice, offers one of these paradigms in a most compelling and fascinating way.

8 Volf, "Systematic Theology," Yale Divinity School, August 27, 2014.

1

MIROSLAV VOLF'S PERSONAL AND THEOLOGICAL BACKGROUND

No thinker creates his or her opus of writings in a spiritual and intellectual vacuum. Miroslav Volf's personality and views materialized not in a void but within certain personal, historical, and ecclesiastical contexts. His personal and theological background shaped his approach to theology and his work in general, and his early life provided the conditions for his understanding of God, church and society at large.

In an extensive interview with me,[1] Volf revealed that his father Dragutin was a Domobran during the Second World War. Domobrans (Croatian Home Defenders) were a Croat political organization that advocated Croatian independence from Yugoslavia, and became associated with the Ustasha regime later during the war. More precisely, Volf's father was a socialist by persuasion and was conscripted when he turned 18, six months before the war ended. He was trained as a baker, and never actually went to the front. Later on he tried to desert to the Partisans (Communist fighters), and his life was spared, unlike his two comrades. He stayed for a while with the Serbian confectioner Dusanovic in Zagreb, Croatia (a boss who was very unkind before the war but generous as a protector after the war), and was then transferred to a labor camp in Slavonski Brod, Croatia, by walking for months in a death march in which about two thirds of those who started the march had been killed off before they ended it. Dragutin encountered God for the first time in that camp. His spiritual experience in the camp shaped his later beliefs and convictions. As a Pentecostal minister he later married Mira and the two of them, according to Volf, found each other in

---

1 Volf, interview by author, Yale Divinity School, July 24, 2014.

1

the context of deep love for God and their mutual striving to be faithful and to serve the church. Miroslav praises his parents' commitment to Christ and their love for the church,[2] which profoundly shaped Volf's character. According to his own testimony, he would never have become a Christian or a student of theology without their inspiration.[3]

Another key person of influence in Volf's early understanding of God was Milica Brankovic, his Serbian nanny, affectionately called Teta Milica (Aunt Milica), who looked after Miroslav in his early age. She became the "angel" of Volf's childhood. Unfortunately, out of negligence she was involved in the tragic accidental death of five-year-old Daniel, Miroslav's brother. Nevertheless, the image of the "angel" remained intact. Volf was ignorant about her role in this incident because his parents, through their forgiving spirit, for a long time covered up her inattentiveness as a cause of this tragedy. Their devotion to Christ was indeed unquestionable. This suffering, however, had a notable worth and a significant influence on young Miroslav.

Remembering his childhood Christian experience in Novi Sad, Serbia, Volf resented both the expectations of sainthood placed on him by the Pentecostal church folk (for whom he was the pastor's mischievous son who ought to know better) and the blatant communist discrimination[4] he encountered in school (where he was a gifted but despised son of "the enemy of the people").[5] Later on he also faced the opposition of the "traditional churches" because he belonged to a so-called sect.[6]

2. Ibid.

3. Volf, *After Our Likeness*, x.

4. "People suffered under communist globalization; I know it from firsthand experience growing up in the former Yugoslavia. A powerful state robbed us of civic freedoms, forced us into mergers of 'unity and brotherhood' in the name of goals we didn't share, disregarded our dreams of 'eating fruit from our own vine and fig tree and drinking water from our own cisterns,' as the prophet of old put it (Isaiah 36:16), despoiled the environment, and trampled on freedom of religion and the right to live our lives as we saw fit." Volf, *Flourishing*, 5.

5. Volf, *After Our Likeness*, ix.

6. "You were politically 'in' if you belonged to the religion/ideology that defined the 'social sacred'; you were 'out' if you didn't. The communists and the leaders of dominant religious groups were in agreement that the 'sects' were out; they broke the ties between religion/ideology and political society. For the sects, allegiance to the one God of all people meant that no political or ethnic group could be excluded from belonging to any particular religious community and that the state should neither seek legitimation from nor offer special treatment to any single religious group; religion and politics are distinct cultural systems. Though my father never articulated even the rudiments of a Christian political philosophy, as a Pentecostal he stood implicitly for a vision of the relation

Therefore, both the loving atmosphere at home marred a bit by the tragedy of the lost brother, and the struggles in the ecclesiastic and social contexts shaped Volf's developing spirituality. He reminisces about the formation of his understanding of God:

> I was born into a faith—well, not actually born into it. My parents belonged to a religious community made up of what the great Harvard philosopher and psychologist William James called "twice born" people, born once of earthly parents, and the second time of the heavenly Spirit. They believed that all human beings required new birth because they've severed themselves from the Source of true life, and they were convinced that a religious community is a voluntary association (what Max Weber called a "sect") that you join after you've been born the second time, not a "family" or a "culture" into which you are slotted just by arriving into this world (what Weber called a "church").[7]

In a public interview done in association with the 2014 Payton Lectures[8] Volf explained that his spiritual life was influenced by both the liberal Free Church and Catholic traditional piety. Even with powerful layers of Pentecostal experience and the genuine Christian devotion of his parents he experienced a teenage rebellion against the church tradition until he was surprised by the power of the Gospel at a large tent evangelistic meeting in Stockholm, Sweden. According to his own testimony, his faith journey was ambiguous. His immature faith was partially challenged by his reading of Bertrand Russell's *Wisdom of the West*, which was very popular when Volf developed his dream of doing doctoral studies in both philosophy and theology. Later on he decided that the trajectory of his work would be to connect faith to broader life. Volf wanted to teach, preach, and pastor the church, but it was one thing to have a gift and another for people to receive it. Church people were not able to appropriate fully his approach to faith, and his dreams were severely undermined.[9] In fact, Volf took courage and

---

between religion, politics, and ethnic identity in stark contrast to the one dominant not just in the former Yugoslavia, but in the entire history of humanity. Although he would never have put it this way, his political stance was pluralist rather than exclusivist, akin to the stances formulated by the English Baptists of the early sixteenth century and later, in an attenuated way, by John Locke." Volf, *Flourishing*, 8.

7 Ibid., 6-7. Volf's footnote on this passage reads as follows: "For the 'twice born' type of religion, see James, *Varieties of Religious Experience*, 73, 121-22, 139-40."

8 Volf, "A Conversation with N.T. Wright, Miroslav Volf, and Mark Labbe."

9. Volf comments on the church's perception of him at this time: "It was less a matter

gave up some dreams. He obtained a doctorate in theology at Tübingen and became part of Roman Catholic-Pentecostal dialogue, but he struggled with the decision whether to stay in Croatia, a space that was not quite large enough to support his theological gifts and activities, or go to the USA to teach at Fuller and work primarily as an academic theologian.

His sensitivity to situations of God's providential leading enabled him to respond and progress. One of these providential events was his talk with a Catholic Church official in Venice, Italy. This man was Raniero Canta-lamessa, the Preacher to the Papal Household since 1980, and a splendid Christian. Volf finally decided as a young man that he would serve this power of the Gospel. Young Volf, therefore, embraced by God, made a firm decision to serve the Gospel of Christ for the common good and in the pursuit of life worth living.

More remarkable still was the way in which Miroslav Volf managed to integrate his personal experience and his spiritual background into his theological opus. His theological background is likewise diverse and rich. His conceptualizations of God and church were developed gradually,[10] and they have never demonstrated the kind of superficiality or mediocrity that is found in some contemporary public theologians. The formative theologians of his early theological development included a group of ecumenical Croatian Catholics (Tomislav Sagi-Bunic, Josip Turcinovic, and others) and Serbian Orthodox theologians (like Atanasije Jevtic and Irinej Bulovic),[11] and one of the key Protestant leaders in Croatia, Peter Kuzmic, who would become his brother-in-law. Throughout his doctoral studies Jürgen Moltmann, his mentor at Tübingen, and Karl Barth (historically and possibly

---

of being perceived as not orthodox enough. After all, I was at that time the editor of the main Christian monthly, read in Pentecostal and Baptist circles. It was more a kind of 'cultural' and 'intellectual' discrepancy. What they needed, I was not best equipped to provide; what I could provide, they were not quite able to receive, at a cultural level. It is almost as if I had wrapping (or jar, to use Paul's language) for the delicacy of the Gospel (treasure would be Paul's word) which people did not like and so they could not eat the delicacy I presented." Volf, to author, May 2015.

10. In a personal communication Volf comments: "My friend, Ivo Novakovic, a truly erudite Baptist theologian now living in Waco and teaching at Baylor, tells me that there are clear and sturdy continuities between my later work as a theologian and my early writings for the Christian magazine *Izvori* which I started and edited between returning from Fuller and going to Tübingen for doctoral work. I have never checked." Ibid.

11 "All Christians found themselves pushing against the same boundaries set by the communists. However, Jeftic would not pray 'Our Father' with Catholics even in the seventies, and I always found that deeply problematic." Ibid.

ecumenically) were the key figures whose theology he absorbed and recon-ceptualized. Moltmann's *Crucified God*[12] and Serbian poet Aleksa Santic's image of "Raspeti Bog" (crucified God)[13] contributed to Volf's understand-ing of the mystery of Trinitarian redemption more than anything else.[14] It took considerable ingenuity to transform these particular rational influenc-es and artistic impressions into something that would become theologically sound and, what is even more important, ethically relevant and appealing.

Deeply influenced by the ecumenical theological framework of both Catholic and Orthodox theologians,[15] as has become self-evident in his ecclesiological-Trinitarian work *After Our Likeness,* Volf still remained faithful to the ethos and theological insights of the Free Churches.[16] To my question about his beliefs or creed Volf bluntly responded that he did believe in the decisions of the first four ecumenical councils and the contri-butions of the Reformed theologians like the young Luther, for example.[17] He discovered the young Luther at Tübingen, translated *The Freedom of a Christian* into Croatian and wrote an introduction to it. Coincidentally, I read this text soon after I became a Christian, not knowing that one day I would be working on Volf's ideas. Luther definitely shaped Volf's theo-logical thought in many different ways. The Reformer specifically became a conversation partner in Volf's notable work *Free of Charge.*

Volf's religious affiliation has been changed, or rather, transformed, as he confesses:

> Over the years I have inched myself into the Episcopal Church, but important impulses in my parents' faith, some widely shared among Christians, have remained with me. *I consider God's relation to human beings and human beings' relation to God to be the condi-tion of possibility for human life and flourishing in all dimensions.*

12 Moltmann, *The Crucified God.*

13. *Kleče mršave Glave Pred likom boga svog—Ištu. Al' tamo, Samo Ćuti raspeti bog.* (Skinny heads are kneeling in front of their god and plead, but there is only the silent *crucified god*—my translation). Santic, "Vece na Skolju."

14. Volf, interview by author, July 8, 2014.

15. Volf, *After Our Likeness*, x.

16. The book *After Our Likeness* grew out of 9 years of Roman Catholic/Pentecostal dialogue at the highest level (including a private audience with John Paul II). Volf, to-gether with the Catholic theologian Herve Legrand, whom he has come to appreciate immensely, was a principal author of the joint statement in 1990, at the end of the 5 years of discussions.

17. Volf, interview by author, July 8, 2014.

> I believe that faith and politics are two distinct cultural systems
> but that an authentic faith is always engaged, at work to relieve
> personal suffering as well as to push against social injustice, politi-
> cal violence, and environmental degradation.[18]

If it were possible to summarize Volf's religious experience and its development, based on the above mentioned inspirations, I could point to
something like a *search for authentic human flourishing and a life worth liv-*
ing based on the reality of God's unconditional and eternal love (from which
follow "justification of the ungodly" in soteriology and "love for enemies" in
ethics) and genuine openness of human beings to transcendence in loving God
and loving neighbor. Volf, of course, completely agreed with this observation. Of one thing we can be certain: his religious experience and his quest
for life worth living have shaped all of his theology and the whole of his
ethical framework. This does not mean, of course, that his theological opus
is purely autobiographical. According to Volf, to "enter into the joy of the
Master" is the ultimate goal of human existence. This joy is "the crown of
the good life, the ultimate goal of all theology. God does not need theology,
human beings do. Humans need theology to help them live the good life, a
flourishing life as beneficiaries and instruments of God's love, as those who
are being pulled 'into the joy of the Master.'"[19]

To sum up, the personality and theology of Miroslav Volf have been
shaped by a variety of religious experiences and ideas. In his pursuit of
relevancy of theology and life worth living his theological opus has become
eclectic. He has borrowed from many sources but refuses to be categorized
as a theologian of any Christian branch. "Volf has the catholicity of a refu-
gee. He's reluctant to join any camp—military, ethnic or intellectual," says
Mark Oppenheimer.[20]

According to Volf's own testimony, it is impossible to view theology
and life from nowhere. Volf admits he writes from a particular vantage
point.

> But the "view from nowhere" is impossible; drones always fly at
> somebody's behest and for somebody's interest. Creatures of time
> and place, we all think, speak, and write from our own vantage
> points, and we do so even when we seek to imaginatively inhabit
> the worlds of others and learn from them. Yet when thinking about

18. Italics added for emphasis. Volf, *Flourishing*, 9.

19. Volf, to author, May 2015.

20 Oppenheimer, "Embracing theology," 18.

world religions and globalization, we inescapably make claims about things that concern all people, their beliefs and practices, and our common life on the planet. This brings authors of books like mine into a predicament: the works are particular but must make universal claims. How have I dealt with this conundrum? Simply: from the place where I stand, I have proceeded to make universal claims about a planetary process called globalization and about other religions.[21]

Volf's vantage point contributes substantially to his universal claims. In several instances he emphasizes that his reflections are not undertaken "from outside historically-given institutions." He does not operate from an "ahistorical transcendent norm."[22] Universal claims are colored and flavored by his eclectic religious and theological background.

From his early childhood, therefore, until his "gradual conversion" with a few remarkable encounters with God, Christian family influence and the enmity of the environment can be traced as determining factors of his spiritual and later religious development. Both his spiritual and theological progress demonstrate the fact that he is profoundly ecumenical in his approach to spirituality and the theology of the church. In his personal and theological approach to God, the church, and the world, the biblically-oriented piety of the Free Churches and the individual assent to God merge with the people-oriented sacramental and communal emphasis of the Catholic tradition. It is not strange, therefore, that Volf is not concerned with doctrinal purity or dogmatic clarity as such. To a large extent his ecumenical theology is more concerned with ethical daily living of the Gospel (life worth living). His theology is conceived as a moral theology that seeks to show not only that Christian faith is intellectually plausible but morally and aesthetically desirable, and "eminently livable."[23]

The religious quest for life worth living brought Volf inevitably to the *ethics of embrace*. The biblical Judeo-Christian narrative of God's embrace, which might include all positive expressions of life worth living in other religions, starts, however, with the tragic reality of our exclusion from God and from one another.

---

21. Volf, *Flourishing*, 18-19.
22. Volf, "Miroslav Volf Replies," 65.
23. Volf, to author, May 2015.

2

ETHICS OF EXCLUSION

REGRETFULLY, DIFFERENT TYPES OF exclusion increasingly define even the most spiritual communities today. Religion, and Christianity in particular, is not immune to this deadly disease of isolation, including self-isolation. The political rhetoric of today's renewed Cold War underlines the isolation of certain nations that do not fit well into the overall world order or the development of globalization. Churches still struggle to bring unity to the divided Christian world.[1] Ideological difference is under threat of being "quarantined." It seems that everywhere exclusion reigns supremely over embrace, and estrangement over acceptance.

Understanding Miroslav Volf's perception of the reality of exclusion is a necessary prerequisite for his conceptualization of the ethics of embrace. The reality of exclusion, according to Volf's unique voice, is first based on the inescapable realities of sin and gracelessness.[2]

---

1. The recent meeting between Pope Francis and Orthodox Patriarch Bartholomew in Turkey recognized the ongoing need for renewed ecumenical commitment based on a common expression of faith, in the face of threats of fundamentalism and martyrdom. Both parties are aware that there are still obstacles to the visible unity of the Christian church, though they signed a common declaration of commitment to full unity. See http://www.cnn.com/2014/11/30/world/europe/turkey-pope-visit/.

2. However, Volf acknowledges that we can truly know what sin is only from the vantage point of its overcoming; or more abstractly, the good helps us identify evil as evil. Volf, to author, May 2015.

Preliminaries: Sin, Gracelessness

> No human being is able to say, of his own and by himself, what sin is, for sin is the very thing he is in. All his talk about sin is at bottom a glossing over sin, an excuse, a sinful extenuation.[3]

Volf's definition of "original sin" in *Exclusion and Embrace* would resemble something like this:

> There is no escape from non-innocence, either for perpetrators or for victims or for a "third party." Pristine purity is irretrievable; it can be regained neither by going back to the beginnings, nor by plunging into the depths, nor by leaping forward into the future. *Every person's heart is blemished with sin; every ideal and project is infected with corruption; every ascription of guilt and innocence saddled with non-innocence.*[4]

In the context of human interactions Volf sees the inescapable inscription of original sin that no one can dispute. This is a prerequisite for every discussion about individual or communal estrangement, alienation or exclusion. Whenever we aspire to do good or dream of a better world we feel this unexplainable, incomprehensible and irresistible power of sin which threatens to drag us down to the depths of inhuman or subhuman thoughts and behavior. Unfortunately, the majority of sermons today lack a deep conviction of sin and consequently the need for atonement and reconciliation. Sinfulness is not taken seriously and most Christians seem to believe that morality or improvement of the character may bring light to this world. But shallow preaching will not lead us out of the darkness of moral self-centeredness and egotism.

Without a doubt, Volf, as a relational theologian, is not so naïve as to claim that all sins are equal,[5] as the perpetrators of evil would like to believe. Nevertheless, he holds that all are *equally sinful*: there is a stain of original non-innocence in every human being and society.[6] The manipulative force of inner corruption makes void every effort or attempt to give, forgive or reconcile with the other. But what is Volf's theological inclination regarding the nature of this original sin? Is it based on the traditional Catholic dogmatic expressions of original sin or on the Reformers' theological

---

3. Søren Kierkegaard, *The Sickness Unto Death.*

4. Italics added for emphasis. Volf, *Exclusion and Embrace,* 84.

5. Ibid., 82.

6. Ibid.

construction of total depravity? His book *Free of Charge* gives us clarity on this: there are no unstained bits in human lives, though we are certainly not all stain and nothing but stain; in fact nobody is all stain and nothing but stain. There is no part which is devoid of original goodness and there is no part devoid of sin; we are good creatures of God and we are sinful creatures of God. Nonetheless, this does not seem crucial for his theological ethics. He is certainly more concerned with the moral and relational implications of original sin than with its ontological essence.

The tendency toward sin is, moreover, reinforced by the fact that we live in the original state of *self-love,* Volf insists. "That's the paradox of self-love: the more you fill the self the more it echoes with the emptiness of unfulfillment."[7] The ethical paradox of hedonism is teaching us that happiness (or pleasure) should not be attained by making it the direct end.[8] The more we desire to please ourselves the more we realize how we become the only center left in the void of spiritual poverty and darkness. It seems as if Volf, in his definition of sin as self-centeredness[9] or "twisted self-love"[10] was reading C.S. Lewis's *Mere Christianity*:

> The moment you have a self at all, there is a possibility of putting yourself first—wanting to be centre—wanting to be God, in fact. That was the sin of Satan, and that was the sin he taught the human race.[11]

This explanation of the essence of original sin is deeply woven into the fabric of Volf's ethics of exclusion. We exclude others when we condemn them, and this is the prerogative that belongs only to God, the ultimate arbiter and the Creator! Should we condemn others? Christ's emphatic *No!* is an expression of His willingness to embrace and save, not to destroy. "For with the judgment you pronounce, you will be judged."[12]

In his book *Against the Tide* Volf does not hesitate to ascribe evil to human beings, contrary to the modern Western tendency.[13] Worse than that,

---

7. Volf, *Free of Charge*, 52.

8 Mill, *Autobiography*, 94.

9. Ibid.

10. Ibid., 97.

11 Lewis, *Mere Christianity*, 53.

12. Matt 7:1.

13. Volf, *Against the Tide*, 27.

"paradoxically, we feel free only in the prison house of *unrecognized* evil"[14] (italics mine). Volf is careful to remind us that we are not *pure* evil, and that we are not in the prison house of evil all the time. However, unaware of the intrinsic hostility toward the true, the good or the beautiful, humanity lives in the optimistic self-deception of religious or secular agendas and programs that lead only to disillusionment and hopelessness. Interpreting Luther in this regard, Volf concludes:

> We sin all the time, blatantly disregarding God and neighbor when we are at our worst, slyly proud and clandestinely selfish in our own achievements when we are at our best, or falsely humble when we see ourselves as unworthy.[15]

Every personal achievement is tainted with sinful corruption. *Free of Charge* deals with this in the personal and individual context, but Volf is equally concerned with the problem of collective guilt and the evil of "new tribalism" and its "blind self-righteousness."[16] This communal, social, religious and cultural self-centeredness leads to vicious conflicts and to different types of exclusion. Many of Volf's ideas, particularly in *Exclusion and Embrace*, are expounded in this ideological context.

Evil is inherently present not only in self-centeredness but in its ultimate results, namely marginalization and segregation. Once we put aside values that come from God's transcendent realm, and the grace that comes from that realm, we are doomed to stagger in the darkness of hatred and self-hatred. The last century has become the clear and convincing evidence that humanity is incapable of resisting the temptation of rejection and exclusion. And at the dawn of the new century this incapability has greatly increased the renewed tensions of nuclear threat and self-annihilation.[17] The sin of exclusion is indeed lethal, and every moral agent in this world should strive towards its complete obliteration. Before I turn to certain types of exclusion, one more preliminary note has to be made.

---

14. Volf, *Exclusion and Embrace*, 90.

15. Volf, *Free of Charge*, 97.

16. Volf, *Exclusion and Embrace*, 37.

17. See, for example, material published by the Nuclear Threat Initiative at *nti.org*.

Gracelessness

Volf clearly indicates that all of our best efforts are tainted with sin. Nonetheless, *gracelessness* is a theological term more used in the context of Volf's social analysis of the gradual disappearance of gratuity and gift-giving.[18] Human beings ontologically are not totally graceless, since we are structurally oriented towards God, explains Volf. What function, then, does religion play? Volf reminds us that in a generic sense, we are all religious because, as Augustine said, our hearts are restless until they find peace in God.[19] Paradoxically, thus, Volf affirms both deep human sinfulness and human ability to resemble the Creator by the free choice of receiving grace. In spite of his appropriation of the Reformed notion of total depravity, Volf argues that human beings generally are on a quest for transcendence and that it is initiated by God's grace, because when we find God we discover that God has already found us.[20]

Consequently, God's relationship to us is different than ours to Him. God has relationship to *all* human beings, and general revelation does exist, asserts Volf, yet common grace is not sufficient in its own right—Christ is always necessary. Volf does believe that all human beings are tainted by sin, though not necessarily through biological or genetic transmission. We are always caught in the sinful condition that subverts and clouds our knowledge of God and therefore we are unable to give and forgive. In his interview with me Volf concluded, "Some can forgive on the basis of common grace because sometimes our practice is better than the theory or the revelation we have received."[21] This is one more convincing evidence that Volf's theology is woven into a fabric of moral pursuit of life worth living.

Gracelessness, stresses Volf in the introduction of *Free of Charge*, is "spreading like a disease throughout many of our cultures."[22] It is "not apparent at first glance, but it nonetheless underlies so many of our interactions."[23] One of the obvious manifestations of gracelessness is "loss of generosity"[24] which "robs us of significant cultural achievements, on

18. Volf, Interview by author, July 8, 2014.
19. Ibid.
20. Ibid.
21. Ibid.
22. Volf, *Free of Charge*, 14.
23. Ibid.
24. Ibid., 15.

which our flourishing as individuals and communities depend."[25] It seems that, for Volf, "the art of giving"[26] is the only proposed antidote to the venomous state of gracelessness. Giving represents the overturn of the natural process of self-fulfillment and self-love. Every gift is a miracle!

In other words, if I wished to underscore the main idea in Volf's ethics of exclusion I would argue that it is his notion of gracelessness, which depicts a life with no personal space for others and no giving—that is, life *not* worth living! We do not *properly* give and we do not forgive, therefore we remain graceless. Lack of generosity paralyzes our willingness and ability to make space for others and to provide help and service where it is needed. Why is it so difficult for us to espouse this quality of giving? The answer is clear: because we tend to exclude, not to embrace.

Types of Exclusion: "I can't breathe!"[27]

Miroslav Volf's deep experience of a severe type of exclusion was a result of his Pentecostal Christian identity in the communist ex-Yugoslavia. His parents, devout evangelical Christians, suffered from the threat and reality of social exclusion. Every member of the Free Church, as I can fully testify myself, was considered a "sectarian" and as such was excluded from the mainstream culture, which was communist or, later, religiously nationalistic. "We couldn't breath!" Nonetheless, Volf argues that the incredible divine embrace gave them strength, and that a hallmark of his family's religion was love for the enemy. Even the madness of ethnic cleansing could not overcome them.[28]

In Volf's ethics, therefore, everything starts with exclusion, but is followed by the possibility of the goodness of embrace. We are born and raised in an environment foreign and hostile to the phenomenon of embrace. In private and public life exclusion seems to be the rule and the only law.

25. Ibid.

26. Ibid., 17.

27 Allusion to a tragic incident in July 2014 with Eric Garner, 43, wrestled in a chokehold by NYPD officers, gasping for breath and later pronounced dead in the hospital. This event sparked protests across US. See http://www.theguardian.com/us-news/video/2014/dec/04/i-cant-breathe-eric-garner-chokehold-death-video.

28 Volf, Evangelical Alliance Interview. Ethnic cleansing is an allusion to 1990s conflicts in ex-Yugoslavia.

Volf brilliantly summarizes different types of exclusion prevalent in contemporary society. First, there is a brutal and warlike exclusion by *elimination*. Second, a somewhat more benign side of exclusion is exclusion by *assimilation*—by a change of identity. Third, there is the exclusion of *domination*—when we subjugate others in order to exploit them. Finally, the exclusion of *abandonment* is negligence in serving the poor or the outcasts, whom we keep at a safe distance.[29]

No Christian would agree that the contemporary church bears the guilt of active elimination or domination, though Christianity's history has some very dark and genocidal moments in this regard (i.e. the Inquisition). The Enlightenment gained ground precisely because Christendom failed to propagate tolerance, and eventually contributed to the spread of exclusion. Speaking about the bigotry of the Christian faith of his times, Voltaire contended: "Of all religions, the Christian is without doubt the one which should inspire tolerance most, although up to now the Christians have been the most intolerant of all men."[30] This graceless conduct seems to be in total opposition to the message of the founder of the Christian faith, and it is rarely the Church standard today.

Nevertheless, exclusion by assimilation or abandonment is deceitfully present in almost every form of institutional religion, including Christianity. Let me share with you what this means by recollecting some very recent experiences in an environment oversaturated with Christian religion but still inclined to exclude by assimilation.

For almost five years I have lived in the Caribbean. Beautiful beaches, calypso music, rum cocktails, and carnival are what most folks have in mind when they think about the Caribbean. Perhaps this is true when one is a visitor or a cruise ship tourist. My personal experience, regretfully, was much different. My Caribbean "career" prospects soon became less and less glittering. When I arrived in Trinidad in December 2009 to teach, unfortunately I was not properly informed about certain crime hot spots, so I rented a house for a while in a very unsafe and not so generous community. Though it did not seem promising, I thought it would be safe. After all, in spite of the cultural alienation my family was yet to experience, the island was paradoxically over-saturated with Christian churches and religion.

---

29. Volf, *Exclusion and Embrace*, 75.

30. Voltaire, "Tolerance," 1. Voltaire explains: "What is tolerance? It is the consequence of humanity. We are all formed of frailty and error; let us pardon reciprocally each other's folly—that is the first law of nature."

Everything was going fine until the night of Monday January 25, 2010. I drove back home late from the University where I was teaching and when I arrived home I opened the car door, leaving the engine turned on while I opened my gate. The moment I wanted to get back to the car a young man appeared in front of me out of nowhere and pressed his gun to my neck. "I can't breathe!" I panicked. In a split second I saw myself dead. With panic I was praying to the Providence to spare my life. Yet, my thoughts were sober. By the grace of God I remained quiet and submissive. Two other fellows jumped into my car and only because I was extremely calm and soundless they did not harm me. They drove off with my car and everything in it. I lost more than 10,000 US dollars; even worse, my Caribbean teaching, my missionary dream, and my divinely inspired project were shattered in pieces. Fear started to paralyze every nerve. Neighbors quickly called the police and they made a report on the spot. The following day I filed the report in the police station, hoping that I would not have to come to that place ever again. In the midst of the subsequent police indolence and corruption, for the first time in my life I felt *totally* helpless and hopeless. I just wanted to go home. I felt alienated and completely *excluded*. The experience left a visible bruise on my neck and a serious psychological trauma. The native folks who were accustomed to this type of incident were indescribably indifferent, but I was indeed grateful to God for preserving my life. This incident made me reflect on the proximity of two different opposite cultures, and the reality of exclusion by assimilation.

The neighbors and my friends later commented that I should not have rented that house or bought that type of car. Well, thank you, I thought! I wondered why no one had mentioned that before. Naturally, we had to move to another safer and much less violent area. My impression was that a certain skin color or foreign presence just did not belong in that community. Coming originally from Serbia, and never having been given a hint of the deep wounds of racism in the Caribbean, I was ready to drift away hopelessly and be forgotten. Following the incident I was tempted to leave immediately for my "good old Europe" but then I remembered rightly that Providence had its own reasons for bringing me to Trinidad. Very soon I did understand these reasons, and I did meet many wonderful people and disciples of Christ with almost impeccable character. They remain my friends forever. I realized I should not have judged God by incidents but by His enduring character and compelling love for me and my family.

Some other later experiences, not so dramatic as that first one, certainly taught me that I had to accept the painful reality of *exclusion by assimilation*: "Either you play our game and belong to us or you will face serious trouble." As a European of a different skin color (in fact I started to live my "whiteness" only when I came to the Caribbean) I had become a target, bearing the strain of being constantly stared at by people evaluating my "whiteness"—I was different from the locals—and much worse, excluding me and my family through the threat of cultural assimilation. Self-awareness was absent. As a friend of my daughter in the elementary school said to her: "I hate white *people*, but I do not hate *you!*" In other words, you have to disassociate yourself from your roots in order to become fully accepted. You have to "color yourself." You have to assimilate! Only if you choose to *belong* either to one or the other community you might be able to receive the Caribbean *identity* (at least in this particular country). Assimilation has become essential for survival. Nevertheless, by the very nature of being Serbian and European we could not assimilate; we could not deny our identity either externally or internally. In fact, I did resist the forceful assimilation for the sake of our uniqueness created by God and our personal background, and for the sake of demonstrating true multiculturalism in the Christian setting.

Being different becomes almost a crime. And oftentimes this exclusion (racial or cultural) is done by the majority's *unconscious* feeling of *necessity* for exclusion propelled by historical inertia or institutional sluggishness. The Christian community is not different in this regard. Difference as it is defined by the mainstream culture simply must not exist—"the territory must be pure!"[31] Serbian soil must belong to Serbs alone (remember *Chetnik*), Croatian soil must belong to Croats alone (remember *Ustasha, Jasenovac*, or "Oluja"), and Caribbean soil must remain Caribbean! Assimilation or death! Exorcism of difference sanctions violence.

Of course, in the historical memory of the post-colonized and post-slavery West Indies, belonging to a certain ethnic group means being a perpetrator and slave owner, or at least a rich squanderer who comes to Maracas Beach every Sunday and associates only with his rich white friends. So perhaps I, being white, did participate in this collective historical oppression.

What about my own exclusion of colored people in Serbia who at least externally resemble certain communities of Trinidad? How often I passed

31. Volf, *Exclusion and Embrace*, 74.

by some Gypsy children, excluding them as non-white, non-Serbian, non-European, people who can never be assimilated and integrated into the fabric of Serbian whiteness! On my last visit to Serbia, in summer 2013, I had a chance to visit some of my elementary school friends. I was thrilled to see them after thirty something years. Surprisingly, I realized that some of them were of Gypsy origin. When we were kids no one really detected this difference, but now, as adults, we tend to exclude, compartmentalize, isolate, differentiate and eventually forcefully assimilate. Even as Christians we do *notice* the difference! Only the miracle of Grace makes us willing to *not* notice this difference and to be willing to fully embrace! Only Grace teaches us to look beyond the visible, cultural, normative, and see a human being in need of embrace.

Moreover, perhaps I bear guilt too for not being able to forgive the boys who attacked me and took my car, or for constantly thinking of myself as a victim, especially when I have a full right to act in retaliation. "I could not breathe!" That was the fact! And, if it were not for Grace, that might have become a reason to detest heterogeneous mixtures of different cultures or races. Perhaps Volf was right when he wrote:

> From a distance, the world may appear neatly divided into guilty perpetrators and innocent victims. The closer we get, however, the more the line between the guilty and the innocent blurs and we see an intractable maze of small and large hatreds, dishonesties, manipulations, and brutalities, each reinforcing the other.[32]

In what ways is Christianity specifically guilty of the sin of *exclusion*? What is the church doing today to prevent exclusion? The following paragraph is the summary of what Volf replied in an interview with me.

Exclusion is a fundamental way in which we sin; it is a sinful way in particular religious communities. This is a temptation for monotheistic faiths and all universalistic religions since we believe in truthfulness or falsehood. This duality subverts the basic message of Christian faith since we are mapping the world according to our cognitive and moral dualities. The grace of God should cross these dualities. It creates bridges. Christ acknowledges sin in the world but he has fellowship with sinners. He names evil as evil but does not condemn an evildoer. The genius of Christian faith is not just morality; it is the forgiveness of sins. Some exclusions are acts of power. Yet, more subtle ones come from a moral coding of the world,

32. Ibid., 81.

concludes Volf, almost twenty years after the publication of *Exclusion and Embrace*.[33]

Thus, if I really wish to embrace the sinner (the other) I have to overlook his or her moral distinctiveness that might threaten my complacency, identity or moral code. Darkness can never overcome light! And darkness is formed not only by our sinfulness but also by our different forms of morality that *exclude* others. Perhaps this is the reason why the Lord of grace was crucified by profoundly moral people! Conventional morality is not in the essence of Christian religious fabric! Grace is! Thank you, Dr. Volf, for this reminder.

Exclusion by *abandonment* is sanctioned even more in the contemporary social structure of distinction between rich and poor (just one example). As Christians, we have to consciously strive to provide the space for acceptance of those who are on the margins of the economic and social structure. Participation is needed, not indifference. Remember Ferguson or Baltimore![34] "I can't breathe!" *My* life matters! "Black lives matter!" Or, as one of the high school black boys who played basketball with me in one of the D.C. parks, asked if he supported or joined *Black Lives Matter* movement, taught me a lesson exclaiming: "*All* lives matter!"

This is always the first step towards the embrace—remember and participate. I will come back to this notion in Volf's discussion of the dynamic relationship between faith and economy. Prior to discussing the ethics of embrace (I haven't said anything about forgiveness yet) let me say just a few words about the consequences of an exclusion mentality.

Results of Exclusion

The underlying assumption of Volf's ethics of exclusion is that it leads to universal non-innocence. "There is no choice. There are no innocents."[35] The primary result of exclusion is that evil has chosen us, not that we have chosen evil,[36] explains Volf.

---

33. Volf, Interview by author, July 8, 2014.

34 Though some claim that Ferguson and Baltimore riots/responses to illegitimate use of force in US (in the cases of Michael Brown or Eric Garner) lead to a high crime era, these responses were legitimate reminders of the crisis of multiculturalism.

35. Volf, *Exclusion and Embrace*, 86.

36. Ibid.

The insuppressible power of evil dominates us. Moreover, the eventual result of exclusion is alienation from ourselves, from God and from the other. As we exclude or become excluded the vicious circle of alienation[37] becomes wider and deeper. We hate and become hated more and more. Finally, we plunge into the unbearable meaninglessness of loneliness and estrangement, and only by a miracle "from above" might we be able to rediscover the meaning of life worth living again. This miracle is called *embrace*.

37 Alienation is a result of all inauthentic human existence based on exclusion (see, for example, sexism as cause of alienation in Rosemary Radford Ruether, "Sexism and God-talk," in Forell, ed. *Christian Social Teachings*, 298-307).

3

ETHICS OF EMBRACE

VOLF'S CENTRAL OVERARCHING THEME, his ethics of embrace, is indeed multidimensional. Aspiring to be authentic in the development of the theoretical framework of this ethics, I have to follow the inner logic of Volf's grand narrative. The ethics of embrace is, in fact, both metaphorical and literal. Reconciliation between individuals, religions, and nations is possible as a final result only by projection of our inner desire or will for resolution, and commitment to *embrace* both as a metaphor and as a tangible reality. The metaphor drives our imagination, aspirations, and expectations, while literally we do come to the point of accepting and actually embracing the other. The metaphor inspires while the physical embrace heals and promotes life worth living. Therefore, I consider *embrace* to be essentially both a metaphor and a literal way of expressing our affection for the other. The more embrace, in both metaphorical and literal senses, the more righteousness, peace, and joy. By virtue of a strict application of the metaphor thoroughly grasped we are able to come to an actual welcoming and hugging of the other.[1]

I believe that Volf's full awareness of this dynamic nature of embrace gives incredible power of influence to his ideas. As a theologian he is both imaginative and practical. He does not leave this metaphor to hang in the air, but gives it a contextual relevance and meaning. He articulates the whole of his theology contextually. Volf's theoretical "system" of the ethics of embrace, based on various theological ideas and spiritual nuggets of

---

1 For those cultures that view hugging as an unacceptable form of greeting, even "light" hugging and keeping distance will demonstrate a desire for embrace. Cultural forms of greeting may vary. Metaphorically, however, wish for embrace is what counts.

wisdom, can be assessed only by following its own reasoning and structure. Let us therefore venture to explore it.

Will to Embrace

According to Miroslav Volf, "joyful embrace"[2] first of all has to be *willed*. Those who are ready to embrace, in spite of the experience of exclusion, have to resist the temptation of giving up. "Despite the humiliation and suffering they have endured, [they] have not given up on *the will to embrace the enemy*,"[3] reminds us Volf in his *Against the Tide*. Despite the deep hurt of exclusion they are willing to press the restart button. In fact, "truth, justice and peace between human beings are unavailable without the *will to embrace the other*."[4] Volf correctly recognizes that the will to embrace is "an aspect of the desire for good implanted in us by our Creator."[5] Therefore, unlike Nietzsche's "will to power" (I believe Volf developed his expression "will to embrace" as counter-Nietzschean), the will to embrace emanates from the original imprint of the *imago Dei*. In spite of the awful ways we have distorted this image, every member of the human family bears the sacred value of human dignity. But additionally, to embrace the enemy, we need to be redesigned in the image of Christ.

In order to practice the embrace one has to be willing first to step out of the comfort zone of the perpetrator/victim relationship. Indifference must be replaced with promotion of the God-given ability to will the good and endorsement of a new set of values. To will to embrace the other means to resolve to reject the self-dependency and complacency that is so often woven into the fabric of our self-centered souls. To will to embrace the other means to die to ourselves—in a way, to will the death of our self-centeredness and to invoke our resurrection as new creatures made in the image of Christ. Embrace is a miracle!

Once we are *willingly* ready to provide the space for the other who harmed us we can move towards the phenomenon of embrace itself.

---

2. Volf, *Against the Tide*, 185.

3. Ibid., 187.

4. Ibid., 192.

5. Ibid., 193-4.

Phenomenology of Embrace

For Miroslav Volf, "the four structural elements in the movement of embrace are opening the arms, waiting, closing the arms, and opening them again."[6] Opening of the arms represents the desire to reach the other and create a space of welcome by invitation.[7] Waiting indicates the fact that the act of embrace is not an act of intrusion or invasion but an act of invitation, of opening the boundary of oneself.[8] Closing the arms is the goal of the phenomenology of embrace and it is reciprocal. Finally, opening of the arms again respects the freedom of the other, who must be let go by respecting the difference and creating possibilities for repeated embrace.[9] But Volf warns that this process is also risky, because I do not know whether I will be misunderstood and rejected in the act of opening my arms. "Embrace is grace, and grace is gamble, always," concludes Volf.[10] Embrace is the ultimate victory over utter gracelessness and lack of generosity. It is *grace abundant* in the midst of *sin abundant*. It is a wonder!

My mother is not a Christian believer. When I made the final decision to be baptized into a Christian community of faith she even fainted and needed physical recovery. She could never accept or even tolerate the fact that my identity had been changed and my inner and outer self transformed. Christ, however, invited us to embrace even those who do not understand our high calling. Even "clumsy" embrace would be helpful. Oftentimes, striving to demonstrate my best self, I have been ready to open my arms in the act of embrace and reconciliation. Perhaps some undercurrents in my inner self and my feelings of abandonment could be traced to my childhood. I am not an expert in developmental and family psychology, but, in regard to the phenomenology of embrace, somehow my mother and I have become stuck in *waiting*. Sadly, confessing my own weaknesses and sinfulness, I acknowledge that I have never been able to close the arms around her neck in the ultimate act of embrace. Waiting has become exhaustive and tiresome, and perhaps even irritating. It is difficult to live in waiting, hoping for the *closing* of the arms—the hope of the weary, excluded wanderer. Perhaps I still lack the essential stimulus that

6. Ibid., 141.

7. Ibid., 141-2.

8. Ibid., 143.

9. Ibid., 145.

10. Ibid., 147.

will propel me to completely embrace my mother as the proximal other? I might make another clumsy attempt next summer. Even this paragraph is clumsy. "It takes knowing the truth to be set free from the psychic injury caused by wrongdoing."[11] What is this truth, Dr. Volf? I would really like to know and clear some new ground for final liberation and embrace.

The Crucifix

What is the ultimate motivation for opening my arms in the act of embrace? For Volf and for all of us, it is knowledge and experience of the perfect wide-opened arms of the Crucified One. He writes:

> We who have been embraced by the outstretched arms of the cru-cified God open our arms even for the enemies—to make space in ourselves for them and invite them in—so that together we may rejoice in the eternal embrace of the triune God.[12]

It was 1990. I got my first ID card and the passport and was excited about traveling abroad. Destination: Palma de Mallorca, the island of Mallorca, Spain. That was probably the most difficult period of my life. I had lost my father as a teenager and by the age of 18 some consequences had become evident. Without God and hope in this life I was searching for meaning in adventure, travel, poetry, art, philosophy, history, and at that moment even in religion. We landed in Mallorca, and from the first day I was interested in tours to Chopin's house, since I loved his music, and, of course, to the great Cathedral of Santa Maria of Palma. The tour of the cathedral was extraordinary. The building was awesome. I noticed the beauti-fully adorned golden crucifix in the middle of the cathedral. Remember, I was not a Christian at that time. I was excluded, not embraced. My interest in religious art was the only reason I walked into the building. Neverthe-less, I was attracted to this crucifix not only as an artifact but as a symbol of my searching for religious experience. As I was closely investigating the crucifix one of my friends asked me if I would like to be photographed with it. I said yes, but before he took the photo I stretched my arms in front of the crucifix, "playing Jesus." Imitating the Crucified! I participated in the crucifixion with my outstretched arms, and how ignorant I was that the scene was somehow prophetic! A year later I got to know Christ in the

11. Volf, *The End of Memory*, 75.

12. Volf, *Exclusion and Embrace*, 131.

military in the midst of war at Prevlaka, Montenegro (now Croatia). One day as I was looking at some photos I found the picture of my outstretched arms in front of the crucifix in the Cathedral of Santa Maria of Palma and I was stunned. The grace of God provided the symbolic prophetic content of my Christian experience long before my actual conversion. I stretched my arms in front of the cross long before the Crucified embraced me with his outstretched arms and taught me to embrace the other. Or perhaps he did embrace me on that day in Santa Maria of Palma, though, in a sense, he had already embraced me two thousand years ago, even in eternity, as "the Lamb who was slain before the foundation of the world."[13]

For Volf's ethics of embrace the cross represents the result of the loving God setting out to embrace the enemy.[14] Christ has created the space in Himself for the offender and the enemy. "The cross is the giving up of God's self in order not to give up on humanity,"[15] declares Volf. The cross has become the central revelation of the triune God since God is love, and in love he stretched out his arms, embracing the unlovable. By grace he accepted the unacceptable.

In the interview "Clumsy Embrace" for *Christianity Today* (1998), commenting on ethnic conflict between Croats and Serbs, Volf offers his understanding of the deep relation between the cross and the ethics of embrace.

> I started thinking about the implications of the Prodigal story for how we relate to one another in situations of conflict, of enmity, of wrongdoing, of suffering. At the center of Christian faith lies not so much liberation, but the embrace of the wrongdoer. That was where the idea of a "theology of embrace" was born. It is simply the Prodigal's father not giving up his relationship with his son—in spite of the wrongdoing of the younger son. When that son returns, the father runs toward him without having heard a single word from that son. He shows his son grace and acceptance because he was and he is and he remained his son even through the wrongdoing. *That is what we see on the cross.* But it doesn't stop there. The God who runs toward us—the wrongdoers—also demands we do the same with those who have wronged us. So there is a social meaning to the cross. Divine grace obligates.[16]

13 Rev 13:8.
14 Ibid., 129.
15 Ibid., 126.
16 Volf, "The Clumsy Embrace."

In the same way, "having been embraced by God, we must make space for others in ourselves and invite them in—even our enemies."[17] The social dimension of the cross is indispensable in Volf's theology. And this creates a fundamental tension which we cannot avoid if we want be the disciples of Christ. Volf summarizes:

> The tension between the message of the cross and the world of violence presented itself to me as a conflict between the desire to follow the Crucified and the disinclination either simply to watch others be crucified or let myself be nailed to the cross.[18]

Can you embrace a *chetnik*? Volf replied with a *tension*. Would he be willing to be crucified for a *chetnik*? One of the questions asked in the *Clumsy Embrace* interview was, "Have you ever literally embraced a *chetnik*?" This is what Volf replied:

> Actually, I've never met one, but if I did I think I would have the will to embrace him, though I also think that much would need to happen before the embrace—a full embrace, an embrace that is not a charade—could take place. Most of us, though, have our own *chetniks*. And yes, I've done the embracing of those who I felt have wronged me deeply. It's hard. It's clumsy to do. It's like God's call to Abraham to "go to a land that I will show you." You have no idea where that land is, but you open your arms and you embrace, unsure about what's going to happen. It takes tremendous courage to do so. It takes practice to do so. It takes self-giving. It also takes suffering. That's the tragic side of it. And yet, in that tragedy there is incredible promise.[19]

Thank you, Dr. Volf, for pointing to the promise of the fulfillment of the unknown; in the crisis of faith and the crisis of hope still the only possible way towards complete reconciliation is through the cross. Would I, as a Serbian victim, be willing to stretch out my arms and be nailed to the cross for an *ustasha* [unrepentant or repentant one?]? Difficult as it sounds, Christ invited us to follow *Him*, not certain convictions or idolatrous images of Him, but Himself as He is, dying at the cross and living at the resurrection. The hope of embrace always lives even in the darkest moments of exclusion—experienced and later remembered. This calls for *imitatio Christi*!

---

17 Volf, *Exclusion and Embrace,* 129.

18 Ibid., 10.

19. Volf, "Clumsy Embrace."

In one of Volf's interviews (2001) in his homeland Croatia he suggested that the example of Jesus is a challenge for all of us, because we are not fully capable of imitating him. Jesus went to the cross of Christ in demonstration of God's love; he did not really care about the preservation of his own integrity, but in giving it up he paradoxically embraced us in love, notwithstanding our wrongdoing.[20] I agree with Volf that the main obstacle to embracing the other (even enemy) is a paralyzing fear of a harmful integrity loss.

Well, Dr. Volf, please tell us finally how important is the Christ event for the ethics of embrace? Christ is the truth, and Christ is the creator, responds Volf.[21] The fullness of God's love and grace is in him. Embrace and generosity happen because God embraces the ungodly. It is also true that Christ's effectiveness is present everywhere where people open themselves up! That is, the Spirit of Christ is present even where Christ is not confessed, and if we respond, if we open ourselves up, we start emulating Christ without knowing it.[22]

The cross of Christ represents, therefore, the platform on which we stand if we wish to embrace the other; when we stand on this podium, whoever we are, there is hope for *total conversion*. What, then, is Volf's position on conversion? In his own work, union with Christ through the Spirit is more fundamental than conversion. He writes:

> Conversion is both the first step toward union and the consequence of the union. Without union, the project remains too moralistic, too much centered on our effort at imitating Christ. Christ, for me, is not first of all a model, though he is a model as well. Christ is the very life through which our embracing of others takes place. Through union, Christ's life becomes ours, both in terms of giving us right standing before God and in terms of giving us ability to live like Christ.[23]

Volf is expressing here what he had already presented in *Free of Charge* and also in *After Our Likeness*. However, he believes that "ethics of embrace" is too narrow as a description of what he is after:

> It is as much *mysticism of embrace*, though the term is often misunderstood. The most important thing does not happen at the level

20 Volf, "21st Century Thoughts."

21. Volf, Interview by author, July 8, 2014.

22. Volf, to author, May 2015.

23. Ibid.

> of our activity in the world, not even at the level of our characters, but at the level of the very foundation of our self—not simply as change in us, but as the presence of the life of Another in us and of our life in Another.[24]

'Mysticism' of embrace, thus, presupposes 'mysticism' of conversion. Time for an interlude.

Conversion

> If anyone thinks he is a Christian and yet is indifferent toward being that, he is not one at all.[25]

The miracle of conversion is the indispensable requirement for the pilgrim's progress towards the fullness of embrace. Abiding faith in the Crucified and Resurrected One gives us the assurance of salvation and the platform to be able to grow in grace constantly. There is no real embrace without complete participation in the "new birth."

What is a conversion? Can we speak about conversion in general terms? I doubt it. Conversion is best understood and becomes relevant only if it concerns particular individuals. Some other questions related to the reality of conversion might be: What are we converted from, and what are we transformed to? Is it a gradual process or a sudden change? Is it a final stage of development of our religious consciousness or an unexpected flash of transcendent light from heaven as in the case of the apostle Paul[26] or Stephen H. Bradley from William James' *The Varieties of Religious Experience*?[27] What is indeed a true evidence and sign against the beliefs of atheists, deists, and agnostics? After all, what is *true* conversion? I have no intention of discussing here the complex theological, philosophical and psychological aspects of conversion, only the experience of the particular individual and her way of life.

Let me go back in my memory and, in spite of serious obstacles and challenges, remember joyfully the miraculous conversion of my sister. I was praying for her conversion for years. In 2003 I went through a time of intense suffering. My sister, who was only 25 years old, was diagnosed with

---

24. Ibid.
25. Kierkegaard, *Works of Love*.
26 Acts 9.
27 James, *Varieties of Religious Experience*, 210-14.

terminal cancer, the result of the complications of FAP, a genetic disease inherited from our father who died at the age of 37. She was not a Christian believer at the time she was diagnosed, but she was living according to healthy principles in the hope that her disease would pass somehow. She went through totally innocent suffering. I did not have an impression of evil of pain quite like Buddha since I knew some of these innocent sufferings before. When I visited her in the hospital the last time before her death (as her brother, but also as her pastor), I still recognized in her an extraordinary desire to live. She was not prepared to die. In fact, who is perfectly prepared to die? As Reza Baraheni, an exiled Iranian poet and political activist, puts it:

> But no one dies in the right place
>
> Or in the right hour
>
> And everyone dies sooner than his time
>
> And before he reaches home.[28]

When I had to tell her that I came to prepare her for death and to call her to commit her life totally to Christ, she still did not believe that it was the end. However, although the doctors said that she would live 15 more days at the most, she lived almost three times as long. During the time she was bedridden, she watched several evangelistic meetings on DVD, committed her life to her Savior and Lord, and was baptized on her deathbed in December 2003 in a celebratory type of the event, exactly 40 days before she died on January 8, 2004. Fully embraced by Christ, she did not have much time to embrace others, but before we left her at the last visit she did literally embrace me and my family, wishing us good health and blessings. She passed away in peace, holding the hands of her family and friends and attentively listening to readings of the Psalms.

As a brother I could not believe that this conversion was so sudden and swift, so I felt like a doubting Thomas. I was not totally sure about her salvation. Was it genuine? Yes, she committed her life to Jesus a few days before her passing, but her whole life was lived in ignorance and sin. Two weeks after her funeral I got the impression, perhaps stimulated by the Spirit of God, that I should go back to the grave and leave my burden of grief there. There was an awful snow storm such as I had never experienced before. In that part of the world snow storms are not common. My umbrella was broken in half. I approached the grave with much difficulty.

---

28 Baraheni, *Mask of Your Limping Murderer*, quoted in Shue, "Torture," 903-13.

As I was praying in this snow storm I felt the unexplained presence of the mysterious and holy Being. The sense of holiness I felt was overwhelming and so intense that I was frightened. The God of holiness and comfort, I believe, sent his angel, who might have been my sister's guardian angel, to assure me that the first sound she heard would have been the sound of the Last Trumpet and the first face she encountered would have been the face of her Savior. Overwhelmed with joy, I left the cemetery with full assurance of her salvation. I was *embraced* by God with a new enthusiasm to *embrace* others. Paradoxically, at the place of extreme loss, I was again ready to live the life worth living and to *give*.

Before turning to Volf's paramount theology and ethics of giving one more autobiographical note.

Giving

"When God gives, God seeks the good of another."[29]

Prior to embracing a Christian worldview I was never taught to give, only to take—not always selfishly and violently, but to receive. I have never held givers to be people whom we should admire. It is true that my father was a generous man but I was not taught to be generous in a proper way. His generosity was ambiguous and dubious. Later I realized that I had a great need of understanding the nature of giving and sacrifice. Yet the truth of giving is not shrouded in abstract thinking but is actualized in concrete acts of service and care.

It seems the call for giving comes in unexpected ways. It was 2003 or 2004, in a suburb of Belgrade, Serbia. I was teaching that day at the Belgrade Theological Seminary and I came back home very late. When I wanted to get out of the car someone was trying to get into the car from a passenger's seat. When I let him in I found that he was full of bullet holes, both in his arm and leg, and blood was spilling all over me and the car. He shouted in despair, "Just drive and I will give you ten thousand euros and that car over there" (a new black BMW on the street). I shouted at him to hold on, and I broke all possible traffic laws to get to the hospital, thinking he might bleed to death. On arrival at Emergency the police detained me for a whole night because they were convinced I was an accomplice in this drug dealers' war. It took the whole night to clear away some misunderstandings. I was

29. Volf, *Free of Charge*, 68.

interrogated for hours. My wife was extremely worried since there was no call from me or any other information during the night. In the morning, when I thought it was over, the victim's brother came to me and searched for some keys, thinking I had a key for that BMW (it was probably full of drugs or money), and his mother offered me money for saving her son. She also embraced me, weeping. The key was already with the police because the victim had dropped the key in my car. Of course, I rejected any compensation for my civil duty and ministry of Christian charity. In danger and crisis I gave without any thought of receiving anything in return. I wanted it to stay that way. The next day when I brought my jacket soaked in blood to the dry cleaning shop the lady bluntly asked me if I was involved in the shooting the previous night. I think I just kept silent, recalling I had a family, I do not remember. Not every form of giving is pleasant. It involves risk and makes us very vulnerable.

My giving was in fact a generous giving *of God* for this man. I was situated providentially in that uncomfortable position in order to learn what giving was. His life was saved. Though it came in an unexpected way, I felt the inexpressible joy of the grace of giving. I felt the bliss of being God's "accomplice" in saving lives by *giving*.

According to Miroslav Volf's ethical stance, giving starts with recognition not of human generosity but of the God of giving. Without the knowledge of the benevolent God there is no stimulus for giving. God is not a negotiator—he does not make deals, he *gives generously*. But, says Volf, neither is God a Santa Claus—when he gives he gives responsibly and *makes demands* of us: God is the Creator who gives generously and unreservedly, but we can wrong God when "we assert our independence, when we ascribe to ourselves what comes from God. That's our main sin against God the giver."[30] On the other hand, the only way to properly receive God's gifts is to open our empty hands for God to fill.[31] This is true faith indeed. Volf has now set the stage for his emphasis on giving by human beings. He reasons, "God's gifts aim at making us into generous givers, not just fortunate receivers. God gives so that we, in human measure, can be givers too . . . God sets the purposes and commands us to realize them . . . God provides the model, and we are ready to observe and imitate."[32] *Imitatio Dei—Imitatio Christi!* If Christ lives in us, we are "Christs" to others.

30. Ibid., 35.
31. Ibid., 43.
32. Ibid., 47-48.

God's giving is our model for what Volf calls the *gift mode* of living. "In the coercive mode, we take illicitly. In the exchange mode, we acquire legitimately. In the gift mode, we give generously."[33] Therefore, we should imitate this mode that reflects the nature of the One who is the "non-receiving giver."[34] God has chosen to give through us. God has not created us to be only receivers, but to be givers as well, concludes Volf.[35]

My giving to the wounded man was God's giving to him through me. God could have done it on his own without human cooperation, but he chose me to participate in giving, and that is a great honor, responsibility and joy. It can happen only if we consent to his providential plan of leading us out of our comfort zone. "Be dressed ready for service, and keep your lamps burning . . ."[36]

Furthermore, Volf explains why a giving attitude is so important for the most profound form of giving—*forgiving* and embrace:

> Good givers are willing to enter the asymmetric relationship with the receiver through their giving without calculation that the giving will pay off. They are good givers precisely because they delight in the presence and desire the well-being of the receiver.[37]

For this reason Volf asserts that we should "give as much to those outside the circle of our intimates as we give to those who are inside it."[38] We should give "without appealing to our self-interest."[39] Giving to a stranger on the street becomes, therefore, as important as giving to our immediate family. After all, who are *good* givers?

Good givers provide *space* for others and are always keen to *embrace* others. Giving is best exercised when it is practiced towards the disadvantaged, outcasts, poor, and underprivileged. Maybe Mother Theresa, Sara Miles,[40] or some volunteers at the European immigrants' camps best understood this principle. Giving, in fact, by definition includes the transfer of something without expectation of receiving something in return. *Imitatio*

33. Ibid., 57.
34. Ibid., 61.
35. Ibid., 79.
36. Luke 12:35.
37. Volf, *Against the Tide*, 169.
38. Ibid., 175.
39. Ibid., 178.
40 Miles, *Take This Bread*. Sara Miles experienced the value of gift-giving to all, irrespective of their religious background or tradition.

Christi seems to be the only possible way of accomplishing this grand and noble calling of transformed humankind. However, the promise of the God of giving is not just based on the call to imitate Christ. Our graceless and sinful nature defies God's generosity and promises. It resists opening ourselves in the act of sacrificial giving. All gift-giving (in the exchange mode) is self-centered, Volf argues;[41] it is a form of getting something rather than an expression of true generosity. The real gift, however, is when you give at least a little bit more than you expect in return, when there is an excess. This ability to give does not depend on what you have; the poor are sometimes proportionally more generous givers because they sense the importance of giving and they depend on the generosity of God. Only the transformative indwelling grace of Christ enables us to imitate Christ in giving a surplus. This theological understanding is the key to spontaneous and generous giving, and Volf's work is a Christian *sui generis* contribution to the theology of giving.

For Volf, however, gift-giving is a preliminary experience for a much more complex, more difficult, more demanding type of giving—*forgiving*. Let me turn now to Volf's profound elaboration of forgiveness as a special kind of gift[42] and as the bedrock of the ethics of embrace. Again, a brief interlude.

Forgiving

It was the end of May 2001. I hate remembering the exact date. My wife was expectant and any day the baby would arrive. The joy of the first child, unfortunately, was eclipsed by a tragic and traumatic experience. Providentially, a few days prior to the incident I walked into the baby's room and was imagining the white cover over the cradle as a cover of death. I was beginning to fear the worst. Like Abraham before the Mount Moriah event, I did not share this insight with my wife. I believe the Spirit of God was preparing me for the days to come. I ignored the thought but confirmation of my fears came. On the Monday morning my wife did not feel any movements of the child at all, and instantly we rushed to the clinic. The doctor was stunned when she realized that there was no heartbeat. We were devastated, and tried to figure out how it could have happened. I even prayed for a miracle of resurrection. Nothing happened. My wife went to the hospital

41. Volf, *Against the Tide*, 178.
42. Volf, *Free of Charge*, 130.

and underwent the awful experience of delivering a stillborn child, and I went home through busy traffic wondering how we would survive this blow. Yet the grace of God did not leave us. My wife received an encouragement from the Scripture that we would receive double for the lost one (we have two beautiful daughters now) and I received the joy of knowing that our little lamb lies in the bosom of Christ. Resurrection, therefore, was just postponed. The baby became indeed "God's first gift" (Mia Theodora was her intended name) preserved exclusively for Himself. The Lord has given, the Lord has taken away![43] And most importantly for us, the Lord has spoken!

Nevertheless, the time came for recapitulation of the experience and some memories of the negligence and carelessness of the doctor came back. We could not forgive her for a long time, though every indicator pointed to a tragic accident. For us, she did not care enough to save our child. Not ignoring the "perpetrator's" responsibility, we should have forgiven at once but we could not. It took some time. This is why forgiveness is difficult. Symbolically, our forgiveness (letting it go) has become Theodora (God's gift) to this undeserving doctor. Forgiving is always gift-giving. Embrace, not exclusion.

Forgiveness is even more complex when, instead of the unknown doctor whom you would probably never meet again, the "perpetrator" is someone very close to you, the immediate family member, a relative, or a friend, or an enemy.

In his interview "Giving Forgiveness,"[44] Miroslav Volf explains the dynamic nature of forgiveness in the context of giving and generosity. He asserts that forgiveness is possible only by crossing the bridge from the self to the other. There are two basic forms of generosity: *giving* and *forgiving*. Forgiveness is the gift to one who is a wrongdoer; it is a different kind of giving. At the heart of all this reality is a gift-giving God who is love by nature, fundamentally a gift-giver. According to Volf, when we forgive we imitate and follow Christ, but it is more than imitation. With God I have a much closer relationship than with the one who merely gives. Volf likes to quote St. Augustine: "In my heart of hearts God is closer to me than I am to myself."[45] Therefore, not only by imitation but by the power of Christ dwelling in us (His intimate closeness) forgiveness is made possible.

43 Job 1:21.

44. Volf, "Giving Forgiveness."

45. St Augustine, *The Confessions.*

Forgiveness, as a special kind of gift, is giving more than the person deserves. I resist, Volf claims, the urge to give back equal measure. In the litigious society of the United States we want to make sure justice is done. If you want to forgive you do not press charges, you look at the person and imagine a forgiven person.[46] I believe Volf had in mind a general Christian stance and not the state's obligation to provide justice.[47]

Forgiving as a special form of gift-giving makes sense in this brief span of human life. Volf recognizes that short-term altruism often aims just to get someone for ourselves. The structure of reality, paradoxically, is made up in such a way that it *makes sense* to give and forgive. As wisdom prevails we need to reach the point of Christian maturity. As already noted, Volf underlines the contrast between God's grace and natural wisdom. At the same time forgiveness is a transcendent gift *and* a coherent and reasonable part of the structure of this already given natural reality. Nature *and* grace, Greeks *and* Scripture, Thomas Aquinas!?

Volf is aware of the fact that forgiveness is often an unfinished product: if a person pushes away the forgiveness, it is still a valuable gift, so even if it is incomplete you have to do it.[48] Furthermore, *forgiveness becomes the echo of God's forgiveness*. Every act of forgiveness is a scandal resembling God's scandalous forgiveness at the cross. No one can deserve forgiveness. Yet unless it happens nothing can be restored. It is a scandal, but also a great need. Volf says in his interview, "If justice rolled all the time, the world would be destroyed."[49] In *Free of Charge* he nicely condenses the broader dynamic nature of forgiveness:

> Forgiveness is a special kind of gift. When we give we seek the good of the other. The same is true for forgiveness: we forgive that they may benefit from the results. There is also a fundamental difference between the two. When we give we enhance the joy of the other in need, but when we forgive we release the other of the

---

46. Volf, "Giving Forgiveness."

47. In Volf's view, the state's obligation to do justice is not the obligation of "retribution" but the obligation to discipline the offender, to protect the innocent, and to underscore publicly the importance of what the crime has taken away, which is to say that it is directed toward the future and is not a repayment for the misdeed. Volf, to author, May 2015.

48. Ibid.

49. Ibid.

burden of guilt. The difference is in violation suffered. That is why forgiveness is more difficult than giving.[50]

The complexity and difficulty of forgiveness stems, therefore, from its unique nature—we deliberately and consciously refrain from searching for retributive justice.

In his interview "Consider Forgiveness,"[51] Volf confirms that forgiveness is risky and tough. We forgive, hoping we will not become losers. Is apology necessary? Well, Volf sees forgiveness as unconditional: that's what God does—He forgives without waiting on us to repent. This is the ultimate meaning of the cross. Forgiveness is not predicated on someone else's apology, but it is not possible to come to fruition without apology. It is like sending a gift to someone—it takes *both* sending and receiving. Have I given a gift to someone who rejects the gift? It depends, replies Volf. It takes another person to receive by apology and repentance.

Why did Volf's parents forgive the negligence involved in the accidental death of his little brother Daniel? Volf remembers that their attitude was based on belief in what the Word of God explicitly *says*. It was very difficult to carry on, but the *purpose* of forgiveness is not to relieve one's own burden or to relieve of guilt of the other but to turn the person to live in a more positive way, even to *flourish*, Volf reminds us without exaggeration probably having in mind his childhood angel, aunt Milica.

Forgiveness comes in droplets and in bits and pieces; dark thoughts come and we realize we do not want to forgive. But we ought to forgive, and we are free to forgive. The *cycle of forgiveness* is always present, explains Volf.[52] It is not a single act of will, it is walking into something unknown and unfamiliar, living in something that develops. As embrace can be clumsy, forgiveness can be too.

Volf's interview "Why Forgive"[53] brings out an additional dimension of his ethics of forgiveness. We cannot remove one's guilt, says Volf. What is needed is to unstick wrongdoing from the doer. It is like a tattoo forever associated with the person, and forgiveness is erasing this tattoo, so to speak. Only God can forgive fully, and it takes a miracle to separate the doer from the deed. The doer dies and is resurrected as a new person, because all have

---

50. Volf, *Free of Charge,* 130.

51 Volf, "Consider Forgiveness."

52. Ibid.

53. Miroslav Volf, "Why Forgive?"

died in Christ.[54] The mystery of forgiveness is hidden in the act in which God took sin upon Himself. Moreover, all humanity vicariously died and were raised in Christ. If we think that forgiveness is desirable and deeply human and should take place, somehow the deed must be separated from the doer, concludes Volf.[55] This unique insight helps us to regard all human beings as *potentially* forgiven and makes our effort of forgiving much easier. Separation of the doer from the deed requires a conscious effort of focusing on Christ's cross-centered method and a constant remembering of the *imitatio Christi* by the grace of God. In the uncharted territory of forgiveness there is a flag post of divine undeserved benevolence, the Hanged and Tormented One.

Elaborating on the complex relationship between justice and forgiveness, Volf admits that this is the question of all questions. It has, of course, two dimensions: intellectual and existential. The existential question is always, How can I live with pain and forgive? First, we should not juxtapose forgiveness and justice. When I forgive I acknowledge that I was indeed harmed! Therefore, how can you forgive if there is no harm? Forgiveness assumes justice: someone did harm to me.[56] In the interview "Consider Forgiveness,"[57] Volf states that some claims of justice are always there when you are wronged and you lose something so dear to you. There is no forgiveness without justice. The best explanation of the dynamic relation between forgiveness and justice is given in "Conversations with Miroslav Volf:"

> Forgiveness is not simply an act that negates justice; rather, it affirms justice in the very act of transcending justice. If I said to you right now, "I forgive you," you would be upset with me and tell me, "There's nothing to forgive, because I've never seen you in my life, and therefore could not have done you any wrong." Clearly I would have blamed you by forgiving you, and it is this sense of blame made against the backdrop of affirmed justice which forgiveness needs in order to be forgiveness. By transcending justice, forgiveness affirms it, rather than leaving it behind. To see justice as a constitutive element of grace is essential to my project, but unfortunately *Exclusion and Embrace* is not always read in that

---

54. 2 Cor. 5:14.
55. Volf, "Why Forgive."
56. Volf, "21st Century Thoughts."
57. Volf, "Consider Forgiveness."

light. Sometimes "embrace" is understood as "sheer gift" without any sense of justice being affirmed.[58]

Justice, or the sense of right and wrong, represents, therefore, the basic presupposition of any type of forgiveness. In the Christian tradition a divorce of justice and grace was always disallowed. The grace of forgiveness presupposes, affirms and finally transcends the sense of justice. Nicholas Wolterstorff contemplates justice which, if understood correctly, might include the act of forgiveness:

> Though Christian scripture speaks often about justice, it neither gives a definition nor offers a theory of justice. It assumes that we know well enough what justice is. What it does do, over and over, is enjoin its readers to act justly and to right injustice. It enjoins them to do so out of a love for justice. It sets those imperatives within a theological context that explains when we should love justice, when we should right injustice, and how we should understand what we are doing when we act justly and right injustice.[59]

To right injustice and to act justly means also to forgive. Forgiveness, therefore, confirms and reflects something of justice. Though it must transcend justice, forgiveness assumes the basic structure of acting justly.

In his 2001 Croatia interview Volf explains another relationship of repentance and forgiveness. He recognizes the fact that confession of sin is more difficult than forgiveness. Forgiveness is complex but repentance is even more difficult. Forgiveness is strength, and repentance is a sign of weakness, but repentance is a condition for freedom. We need repentance to recognize failure.[60] To repent is the most difficult Christian experience, insists Volf. Forgiveness assumes power: I am the one who is right. In repenting, however, I am standing exposed and I do not know what is going to happen to me. Volf observes that Pope Benedict XVI [or currently Pope Francis] made a right move when he pointed to sin *within* the Church. We *all* need repentance.[61] Especially those who claim they are depositors of the grace of God.

Can we forgive the perpetrators that demolished our sense of self-esteem and self-worth? Regarding the atrocities in the Balkan wars and the

---

58 Volf, "Conversations with Miroslav Volf, part 2," 84.

59 Wolterstorrf, *Journey Toward Justice,* 69.

60. Volf, "21st Century Thoughts."

61. Ibid.

particular context in which both Volf and I were raised, there was and is much to be forgiven. But with wrongful memory forgiveness does seem implausible and impossible. Volf indeed confesses: "I cannot embrace the *chetnik*, but as a Christian I should be able to do that!"[62] And then, here at Yale, 13 years later I asked Volf, "Why can't you embrace a *chetnik*?" (This was an allusion to the 2001 interview.) "Was it a political statement or a heart statement? You said you *should* be able to do that. Haven't you just embraced a *chetnik* when I stepped into your office?" I challenged him with a smile.

Chetnik is a metaphor, Volf responds.[63] A *chetnik* is someone who is a *present* source of harm, or who has been a source of harm. Well, Dr. Volf, let me ask you another question: should the Croatian nation apologize for Jasenovac and Oluja, and the Serbian nation for atrocities in Slavonia and Bosnia, and should this be the starting point of reconciliation? At the level of nations and ethnic groups this is a very slow process, admits Volf. What is needed is *transparency*, truth commissions, common writing of history, and purification of memory. All of this might contribute to further reconciliation. Emphasis only on unqualified *remembrance* is not helpful, because if we do remember we have to do it well and rightly in order to forgive, concludes Volf.[64] Later on I will refer to Volf's work *The End of Memory* as a foundational opus for the understanding of remembering rightly. For now, I admire Volf's courage to respond to my sensitive questions that make historical and individual harm and forgiveness so tangible that we could feel it on our skin.

There is one more note worth mentioning before I turn to the meaning of rightful or proper remembrance in the same context of forgiveness and the ethics of embrace. How does forgiveness work with other religions in comparison to the Christian faith? According to Volf, Buddhism has compassion but forgiveness is different; Islam and Judaism have different approaches as well. The Christian theology of forgiveness is based on the principle of *unconditionality*. It is prior even to a person's need of forgiveness. Before I was there, God in Christ took my sin away and reconciled me to Himself. His forgiveness just needs to be received. When the gift of forgiveness is not received, forgiveness is not complete. Central for Volf is to look at forgiving as a social event—not as something that happens merely in a person, but something that happens between persons. Forgiveness is a

---

62. Ibid.

63. Volf, Interview by author, July 8, 2014.

64. Ibid.

movement, in which there may be a partial instantiation of forgiving even if there is not fully fledged forgiveness. Forgiveness may be partial partly because we find it difficult to forgive and partly because the other person may refuse to accept forgiveness.[65]

Volf always starts from the presupposition that we are recipients of abundant gifts of God's grace in Christ.

> Just as divine grace invites to repentance and makes repentance possible, so also victims' gift of forgiveness creates a space for perpetrators to admit their fault, ask for pardon, and mend their ways.[66]

In fact, God's commitment to forgive the world comes before creating the world. The God who gives is the one who forgives. Similarly, in marriage, for example, the commitment to forgive comes before the marriage vows.[67] "The same love that propelled God to create by giving propelled God to mend the creation by forgiving."[68] "For Christians, forgiveness is paradigmatically enacted in Christ's death."[69] The cross stands as the ultimate fulfillment of the unconditional and prior gift of universal forgiveness.

God condemned sin universally in Jesus Christ. "God did so not out of impotence or cowardice, but in order to free us from sin's guilt and power. That's how we should treat those who transgress against us. We should absorb the wrongdoing in order to transform the wrongdoer,"[70] contends Volf. Contrary to revenge that multiplies evil and retributive justice that contains evil, forgiveness overcomes evil. "The heart of forgiveness is relinquishing retribution."[71] It seems, according to Volf's ethics and theology of forgiveness, that those who seriously immerse themselves in the free gift of God's unconditional forgiveness are able to offer the same gift to others. His insistence on complete "letting go," "absorbing" the wrongdoing and transforming the perpetrator implies that only radical disciples of Christ and committed followers of the ideals of the Sermon on the Mount are capable of genuine forgiving. A natural theology of forgiveness, therefore,

---

65. Volf, to author, May, 2015.

66. Volf, *Against the Tide*, 172.

67. Ibid., 55.

68. Volf, *Free of Charge*, 141.

69. Volf, *The End of Memory*, 111.

70. Volf, *Free of Charge*, 161.

71. Ibid., 171.

has no place in this dynamic and transcendent reality. Unless Christ does the forgiving through us, we cannot walk this road.

Finally, speaking about embrace as an *outcome* of forgiveness, Volf explains:

> Forgiveness places us on a boundary between enmity and friendship, between exclusion and embrace. It tears down the wall of hostility that wrongdoing erects, but it doesn't take us into the territory of friendship. Should those who forgive stay in a neutral zone?[72]

He adds, "There can be no embrace of the former enemy without forgiveness, and *forgiveness should lead beyond itself to embrace.*"[73] And, I would certainly add, to life worth living! Forgiveness "lets the offense slip into oblivion not right away, but eventually, not as a matter of course, but when the time is ripe."[74]

When the time was ripe my wife and I forgave the negligent doctor. But we should be able to *embrace* her as well. After all, she is like us, co-sufferer and co-searcher for Christ. One day we will hug her, not just metaphorically. Every forgiveness leads to embrace. There is no neutral zone! The cross of forgiveness leads to the joy of ultimate embrace.

Giving, and forgiving the offense, is undoubtedly at the center of the ethics of embrace and the fruitful life worth living. But how is it possible not to remember the offense any more? How can we move beyond forgiveness to the ultimate act of embrace? Perhaps also by remembering rightly!

Remembering Rightly

Remembering wrongly or rightly? I always remember my father as a stern disciplinary figure who possibly crossed the line between love and discipline. Perhaps he had no chance to learn it from his own father. He was raised in a poor, hardworking family. I remember my father as an abusive alcoholic who, wishing a good future for his son, suddenly abstained from alcohol. By human effort and common sense he did his best to mend his ways and serve his family. There was another ray of light in this dark memory. Recalling the last moments of his life in the hospital always brings

72. Ibid., 188.
73. Ibid., 190.
74. Ibid., 173.

me despair and hope at the same time. He was dying of a terminal genetic disease and he had no time or energy to talk to us children. I was 14 and my sister was 8 when we visited him in the hospital for the last time. In that moment when everything was hopeless he demonstrated caring love and fear for our future by telling us to be obedient to our mother and to respect her. Was his *sensus divinitatis* working properly? After the painful death of my father and the awful cold winter funeral, I experienced desolation and agony, and I was giving my best to keep my emotional machinery working well enough to propel me forward despite all. Yet, the ambiguous image of my father called for clearing out of my memory.

So, do I remember wrongly or rightly? How can I remember rightly? Is my mind still enslaved by the abuse or neglect I suffered as a child?[75] To what extent did my father colonize my future and eclipse the horizon of my possibilities?[76] Will he always be an abusive alcoholic even in my nightmares?[77] What about the change in his character—where does that fit into the picture? Is there any hope in remembering rightly?

The key question posed by Miroslav Volf is: "How should I remember abuse as a person committed to loving the wrongdoer and overcoming evil with good?"[78] In Christian faith this is the cornerstone of practical expression of religious belief. Remembering properly is an integral part of the forgiveness experience. There is, indeed, a need to remember rightly. Only by remembering rightly there is a hope in forgiveness, reconciliation and embrace. Volf's volume *The End of Memory* came as a "good medicine for our cultural health and personal flourishing."[79]

First of all, according to Volf, the memory of pain replicates pain.[80] Memory is a part of our identity, so pain becomes part of that too.[81] Therefore, the blessed life should include forgetting how suffering and evil *felt*.[82] Life worth living cannot be interpreted and attained without remembering rightly. The bottom line is the following:

75. Volf, *The End of Memory*, 7.

76. Ibid., 12.

77. Ibid., 16.

78. Ibid., 11.

79. Ibid., 232-33.

80. Ibid., 21.

81. Ibid., 24.

82. Ibid., 23.

> Victims will often *become* perpetrators precisely *on account of* their memories. It is *because they remember* past victimization that they feel justified in committing present violence . . . So easily does the protective shield of memory morph into a sword of violence.[83]

Thus, remembering rightly would bring not just healing for the victim but the breaking of the cycle of revenge and perpetual violence. It was Gandhi who said, "An eye for an eye only ends up making the whole world blind." It is critical to know at this point that revenge or retaliation is sometimes directed towards the innocent party and has nothing to do with the original perpetrator. How many nominal Christians, raised in abusive families, continue to abuse their spouses or children because they remember wrongly? Isn't this an urgent call to forgiveness in remembering rightly?

Well, Dr. Volf, doesn't forgiveness as forgetfulness or the lack of memory cover up and promote further violence of the perpetrator? Isn't memory, though ambiguous, still the redeeming keeper of moral equilibrium, as Elie Wiesel said: "Because I remember, I despair. Because I remember, I have the duty to reject despair?"[84]

I do not like the expression *forgetfulness*, Volf responds in his interview with me.[85] *Non-remembrance* or *not coming to mind* is a better expression, and this reality is possible as a conclusion of successful reconciliation, not as a condition for reconciliation. Forgiveness is a social event between people. Forgiveness will stimulate the slow fading of the memory of the perpetrator.[86] Is it still a process or it is final? Forgiveness is a process and where we are in a process determines how good the chance is to be transformed. It is a life journey, Volf reminds us. Religious imagination is one thing but reality is another. Appropriation should be done in Christian terms and we need Christian-motivated imagination. Forgiveness is dealing with our own resentment but it is much more about reconstituting relationships with people. Forgiveness aims at returning to the other their own good from which they have fallen. Volf notes that this idea is expressed by the young Luther, but it is inscribed into the logic of salvation.[87]

Volf's conviction about forgiveness, therefore, presupposes a certain anthropological model, namely personhood that is always in search

---

83. Ibid., 33.

84. Wiesel, "Hope, Despair and Memory."

85. Volf, Interview by author, July 8, 2014.

86. Ibid.

87. Ibid.

of holistic relationships. Forgiveness provides the space for restoring this basic nature of all human beings. This remarkable idea is, indeed, fresh, vibrant and illuminating. *Shalom* is impossible without forgiveness! The common good and the ethics of embrace are possible only if we forgive by remembering rightly!

Volf reminds us that when we remember we also tend to reconstruct events, sometimes untruthfully; in fact, we are faced with the impossibility of remembering truthfully.[88] Victimized and hurt, we have unintentionally distorted memories of the past. This distortion may paralyze our ability to forgive and receive forgiveness.

The solution that Volf offers lies in remembering through the lenses of the sacred memories of the biblical Exodus and the Passion of Christ. These memories bring healing and a new form of participation. It is difficult, however, to be "a Christ" to the neighbor and remember rightly. For this reason we need to *participate* in the community which supports the remembrance through the lens of the Passion.[89] The theological significance and religious experience of the Passion of Christ can transform the community, which becomes enabled to forgive and remember rightly. The Church should embody Christ's graciousness and forgiveness.

Volf's argument is not that memory is bad and amnesia good, or that forgetters have a comparative advantage over rememberers, but rather that *under certain conditions the absence of memory of wrongs suffered is desirable*.[90] How can I embrace a Croatian today if I constantly have Jasenovac in front of my eyes? My memory of atrocities can be suspended by my desire to terminate the vicious cycle of retaliation and to promote peace and love. This is true both individually and collectively. It is not just concern for ourselves, but also love for the other, that constitute the reasons for letting go the memories of wrongs suffered.[91] Loving others is the miraculous fruit of the continuing remembrance of the Passion of Christ (the ultimate loving of the other), and therefore, absence of memory of wrongs suffered is possible only by perpetual commitment to the One who said, "I, even I, am he who blots out your transgressions, for my own sake, and *remembers your sins no more*."[92]

88. Volf, *End of Memory*, 61.

89. Ibid., 126.

90. Ibid., 148.

91. Ibid., 165.

92. Isa 43:25 (NIV).

Therefore, at the Last Judgment I do believe that my father will receive what Volf calls an "actual acquittal."[93] Me too, because I was neither a perfect son then nor a perfect father now! And I also believe that we will be absorbed in a piece of arrestingly beautiful music—music that captivates our entire being and takes us on an unpredictable journey.[94] This journey of *life worth living* starts now and will continue with *embrace* as it becomes a journey of a new transcendent form of *love*!

Love

> Love is not a warm feeling, though warm feelings may accompany it. At its core, love is not feeling at all, but an action, a way of being, in active care for others—for the integrity of their bodies and souls, as well as for their flourishing.[95]
>
> If anyone has material possessions and sees his brother in need but has no pity on him, how can the love of God be in him?[96]

My wife, coming from a Christian family, indeed helped me greatly to understand what it means to love and care without asking anything in return. Both in my marriage and my Christian experience I had to absorb Christ's offer of unconditional love that I was almost ignorant about. My wife has become one of God's primary instruments for assisting Grace to transform me to love unconditionally and to demonstrate love by active care. I would have seemed a loving but sometimes distant figure to her, given the demands of life and ministry. Distance was an everyday imperative in my original family—not hatred and rejection, just distance with indifference. But I made a conscious effort to love my present family. I willed to love. My wife's strength and evident maturity in dealing with family issues and children is an inspiration to me to continue to support and show love to her and the children unconditionally. Though I am still learning how to love, I bask in our love. Love that cares and promotes mutual flourishing was revealed to me and infused in me by Christ and, in a tangible way and instrumentally, through my wife as well. This love and embrace might be clumsy sometimes, but my inherited feeling of distance gave way to a feeling of

93. Volf, *End of Memory*, 229.
94. Ibid., 230.
95. Volf, *Against the Tide*, xi.
96. 1 John 3:17 (NIV).

acceptance and being accepted. Desire to embrace fully has become a desire to love unconditionally. Thomas Jefferson's statement that "harmony in the marriage state is the very first object to be aimed at"[97] indeed prompted me to think about the importance of the most intimate relationship we have in this world. Once I realized that, I also strived towards embracing and being embraced through unconditional love, which in marriage has the threefold expression of *eros* (loving the other for the sake of myself—pleasure and fulfillment), *philia* (loving the other for the sake of the joy of the relationship of friendship) and *agape* (the divine form of self-emptying love—loving the other for the sake of the other).[98] Love of the body, love of the soul and ultimately love of the spirit together demonstrate active care and promote flourishing. And even this highest human expression of love is just a dim reflection of the transcendent universal divine love.

For Miroslav Volf, the ethics of embrace is primarily based on the ethics of love. Both in *Captive to the Word of God*[99] and in *Allah*[100] Volf elucidates the idea of God as Love and its implications for personal and communal ethics. Volf starts with a Christian definition of God's love:

> Because God is the Holy Trinity, God's eternal love can be self-giving love rather than self-centered love. Consequently, God's love for humanity is a freely given love rather than a love motivated by the benefits that the object of love holds for the one who loves it.[101]

Quoting Martin Luther, Volf concludes that "objects do not elicit God's love by their qualities; God's love creates objects together with their

---

97 Meacham, *Thomas Jefferson*, 51.

98. Apart from the historic Christian discussions on the nature of love by such as Augustine, Calvin, Luther and Kierkegaard, one of the best comprehensive peer-reviewed articles on the nature of all three forms of love is "Philosophy of Love" by Alexander Moseley in the Internet Encyclopedia of Philosophy, at www.iep.utm.edu/love/.

99. Volf, *Captive to the Word of God*, 140-50.

100. Volf, *Allah*, 163-84.

101. Volf, *Captive to the Word of God*, 140. According to Volf's Evangelical Alliance interview, the identity of Christ makes all of us Trinitarian. This is a very difficult doctrine but it is also beautiful. For Volf, the love and community of the Trinity is the pattern for the ecclesial community (Volf, *After Our Likeness*, 191). For his ecumenical work on the Trinity and the church, see *After Our Likeness*; this deals primarily with an evaluation of ecclesial individualism and classical Catholic and Orthodox forms of ecclesial holism, and offers an alternative based on the proper understanding of the Trinity, namely more nuanced relationships between persons and community.

qualities."[102] God, therefore, seeks to "recreate the object to become lovable again."[103] Unlike other religions except perhaps Judaism, Christianity always affirms that "love is God," that is, "love properly understood *is* God," and that "God properly understood *is* love."[104] Volf describes God's love as immeasurable, utterly gratuitous, completely unconditional, universal, and indiscriminately forgiving.[105] The list of attributes of God's *agape* love is inexhaustible. With a revelation of God's love that transcends our comprehension, we admit that our "cognizing" is based on the Socratic principle: now I understand that I don't understand. We also desire to love as we realize that love is the meaning of life worth living. As Augustine says in his *Confessions*: "I was not yet in love, yet I loved to love . . . I sought what I might love, in love with loving."[106] Following a discussion on the nature of love in Islam and Christianity, Volf concludes:

> For Christians, that's where the Trinitarian nature of God comes in. From eternity to eternity, God's love is not self-love, but a self-giving love. It is God's nature to give. That's why God gives even to the unrighteous. Love for the ungodly is the shape that God's love for the divine "other" takes when faced with godlessness.[107]

The Christian description of the God of love, unlike the Muslim concept,[108] includes God's command to love even the enemy. It is not just kindness to all; it is the imitation of God who *loves* the ungodly. And this becomes the most important implication of Volf's ethics of embrace based on love. Volf accentuates this:

> God loves, therefore, we must love; God is love, therefore we must "be" love—delighting and correcting, supporting and resting, and at all times benevolent, beneficent, and actively caring love.[109]

Dr. Volf, I understand that love is crucial in understanding God's nature and the nature of embrace. To "be" love transcends mere acts of love. Nonetheless, the contemporary society needs some other metaphors

---

102. Ibid., 141.
103. Ibid.
104. Volf, *Allah*, 165.
105. Volf, *Captive to the Word of God*, 142-43.
106. Augustine, *Confessions*, 3.1.1.
107. Volf, *Allah*, 176.
108. Ibid., 182-3.
109. Volf, *Captive to the Word of God*, 147.

to express the nature of love. How should we speak about love in contemporary terms without strictly religious language?

Gift giving is a metaphor for love, replies Volf. Love is when we give a little bit more than expected.[110] In "being" love or loving to love, therefore, we are transformed in order to give, forgive, remember rightly and embrace the enemy. "The way of being" love promotes the flourishing of others and therefore promotes the common good and life worth living. *The life of love is a life worth living*. It is truthful, beautiful and good. The ethics of embrace is best understood in the context of this abundant and forgiving love. Ultimately, only those who follow the way of being in love can embrace the whole world. As Kierkegaard said: "When one has once fully entered the realm of love, the world—no matter how imperfect—becomes rich and beautiful, and consists solely of opportunities for love."[111]

So far I have explored the individual Christian calling to give, forgive, embrace, and love in active care. Now I would like to explore how this power of love is best demonstrated in the public arena. Volf's ethics of embrace based on unconditional forgiveness and love turns out to be valid also for the ethics of public faith and the pursuit of life worth living, and the most compelling testimony to our loveless, faithless, graceless, weary and waning world.

---

110. Volf, interview by author, July 8, 2014.
111. Kierkegaard, *Works of Love*.

4

ETHICS OF THE TESTIMONY (PUBLIC FAITH)

Public Faith

> If we can neither state what the gospel is, nor have a clear notion
> of what constitutes the good life, we will more or less simply float
> along, like jellyfish with the tide. *True, a belief in our ability to
> shape the wider culture is woven into the fabric of our identity.* So
> we complain and we act. But in the absence of determinate beliefs
> and practices, our criticism and activism will be little more than
> one more way of floating along.[1]

FINDING THE WAY TO present Christian values in the public sphere is one
of the fundamental tasks of Volf's theology and ethics. He is concerned,
first of all, with the proper function of religion in the public arena. Volf's
A Public Faith exhibits this function in a most comprehensive way. It is not
misrepresenting Volf's plan to say that this is his primary project. In his
ethical and theological framework Volf is searching for the unique Christian vision that will be able to dialogue with other religions and transform
the world as well.

Because of certain malfunctions of faith, the Christian religion (along
with other religions) fails to exercise public engagement in a proper way.
Faith that is idle[2] or coercive[3] is destructive in any attempt to participate

---

1. Volf, *Against the Tide*, 142.
2. Volf, *A Public Faith*, 13-17; 23-36.
3. Ibid., 17-31, 33-54.

in public life, argues Volf. If faith is emptied of its meaning, purpose, and power, or violent and oppressive, it cannot function properly and it is totally misused. This happens when the faith we embrace has nothing to say about how we should conduct our lives in spheres such as the economy, politics, arts, security, and others, when believers find themselves constrained by foreign systems of life and work, and when faith is not applied to new circumstances and does not seem relevant to the contemporary world.[4] Moreover, Volf argues that religion malfunctions when it is related to a certain group or to economic success or the flourishing of religion.[5] Consequently, it betrays transcendence and universal commitment. It becomes just service, a mechanism for success, and faith is idling.[6] Idle faith, therefore, ultimately denies its very purpose, namely, active transformation of the world. Eventually it becomes totally irrelevant and in some cases obsolete and dead, in spite of its attempts to live on through certain immanent institutions.

In his interview "Public Faith," Volf first explains that we live in a pluralistic world in which we need to bring Christian faith vision. Malfunctions of faith are the result of faith being inserted into the world in inappropriate ways. A brilliant observation of Volf reveals that we are not always purely coercive or idle; rather, we oscillate between coerciveness and idleness. The presence of faith in the public arena, therefore, is ambiguous.

In this same interview Volf asks: How should we bring faith into the public realm and shape public sensibilities? First of all, we need the *character* of Christ, and second, as we are shaped by Christ, we start thinking about the broad vision, namely *God's vision* for the world and its response to God who is love. The purpose of a Christian vision is to bring to the world a vision of what it means for human being and communities to flourish. We need to initiate dialogue with other faiths, basing it on the discussion of what it means to *flourish*. This would be a great contribution to the common good, concludes Volf.[7] It is important that Volf never offers nominal definitions but real ones, and his analysis masterfully reveals the essence of the problem. To be ethically relevant every religion must participate in the public arena in its own way. The multiplicity of methods of participation in the public arena makes it possible for every religion to contribute in

4. Ibid., 23.

5 Volf, "Life Worth Living."

6. Ibid.

7. Ibid.

vibrant and dynamic ways. Volf rightly recognizes that the common good should always be the ultimate goal of this vividness and non-coerciveness of religious sentiment. Christians, therefore, should exert strenuous efforts in refusing to let their faith become idle. It will make a positive difference only if we recognize that God is the source of blessing, liberation, guidance, and the meaning of everything we do.[8]

Coerciveness of faith, on the other side, is caused by "stripping Christian convictions of their original cognitive and moral content and reducing faith to a cultural resource" with "an aura of the sacred." This will inevitably inspire and produce violence.[9] Every form of religious fundamentalism draws its energy from this principle of coerciveness. When universal and transcendent moral/spiritual content is strengthened, fundamentalist claims to religious cultural exclusivity are weakened.

The solution, for Volf, lies in "building bridges between religious cultures estranged on account of violence that was triggered largely by nonreligious motives."[10] Finally, Volf settles the matter:

> Properly understood, the Christian faith is neither coercive nor idle. As a *prophetic* religion, Christian faith will be *an active faith*, engaged in the world in a non-coercive way—offering blessing to our endeavors, effective comfort in our failures, moral guidance in a complex world, and a *framework of meaning for our lives and activities*.[11]

This seems to imply that the ultimate result of this prophetic faith will be human *flourishing* or life worth living, and the secret of this flourishing is the presence and activity of the God of love who can make us love our neighbors as ourselves.[12] The unique moral vision of Christian faith becomes, therefore, public moral guidance. This has to be explored further.

To my question, "What is the nature of prophetic faith?" Volf answers that prophetic faith is faith that is engaged both privately and publicly to transform lives at both levels. Unlike mystical religion that strives for the seclusion of the soul with the divine, prophetic faith aims to *shape* reality. Religious experience, notwithstanding its transcendent goals, finds its place in the midst of mundane realities. There should be an alignment between

8. Volf, *A Public Faith*, 36.

9. Ibid., 51.

10. Ibid., 54.

11. Ibid.

12. Italics added for emphasis. Ibid., 74.

the interior life and external behavior, and both should be aligned with Christ's life, insists Volf. Prophetic faith is simply shaping cultural sensibilities, concludes Volf, but public engagement should take place in ways that recognize that a Christian vision of the good life is not the only one that respects other people and their attempts to bring their visions of the good life to bear on public life. Prophetic faith also pushes for political conditions in which all people, with both religious and non-religious interpretations of reality, can be engaged publicly on equal terms.[13] Hence, every religion in the public sphere can and should serve the common good, and the highest good of all for Volf is the flourishing of humans, living a life that is worth living.[14]

Flourishing seemed to be a new idea in Volf's theology, so I inquired why it is so critical for the common good. The term *flourishing* is a metaphor from the natural world, Volf explained. It applies not just to cognitive well-being but to *general* well-being. The three characteristics of a flourishing life are that it goes well (one's circumstances are good), it is being led well (one's interior and exterior activities are good), and life feels good (one has a sense of happiness, contentment, or, more properly, joy). One's flourishing can be subverted, continued Volf, but joy comes as we properly read the circumstance. Objective conditions are relevant but they are not enough to define the life of flourishing.

Nonetheless, I asked, doesn't the discipleship of Christ and His cross seem to contradict the philosophy of flourishing? What kind of flourishing are you speaking about? Well, continued Volf, the cross is not a masochistic tool. Bearing the cross should bring about the state of affairs which corresponds to *movement towards flourishing*. That is why the complex reality of flourishing life is fulfilled even when one dies at age 33 on the cross, explained Volf.[15] Of course, Christians also have a hope of resurrection, Volf reminds us. Both the Garden of Eden and New Jerusalem imageries point to personal and social flourishing of life that goes well, that is led well, and that feels good.[16] The meaning of *joy* in religious experience is

---

13 Volf answers that there are varieties of proposals of what it means to be a human being. There are multiplicities of self-social relations and the good we aim at. Religious experience should be aligned with mundane realities by transcendent goals, insists Volf. Interior life should be adjusted to external behavior.

14. Volf, Interview by author, July 8, 2014; Volf, to author, May 2015.

15. Ibid.

16. Ibid.

also currently being explored by a new initiative of the Yale Center for Faith and Culture.[17]

Another dimension of the flourishing life worth living is based on the fact that Volf's account of public faith endorses not only a theoretical or existential loving of God and neighbor but the practical implementation of some aspects of political liberation theology or liberation of the poor. At least some scholars believe so. M.T. Dávila noticed that in Volf's approach to public faith, he "echoes many liberationist sensitivities."[18] It is indeed impossible to talk about flourishing without the vision of liberation within every aspect of human existence alienated from its original purpose. Jean-Paul Sartre would probably feel nauseous over this comment of mine. But human nature without the original purpose cannot be alienated and estranged. Only in that context liberation and pursuit of flourishing could have some meaning.

Volf explores the issue of flourishing much more deeply in his most recent volume, *Flourishing: Why We Need Religion in a Globalized World.* Let me bring this discussion on public faith and its relevance for the common good to a close by quoting Nicholas Wolterstorff's brilliant summary of *A Public Faith:*

> Authentic Christian engagement seeks neither to abandon society nor to dominate it; it seeks rather to make a difference, saying "No" where No must be said and "Yes" where Yes calls to be said, sharing Christian wisdom while being open to the wisdom of others, seeking the common good by working with others for the common good, acting always out of love for God and neighbor.[19]

In my humble opinion the only way that this authentic Christian engagement of the prophetic faith functions properly is to provide and proclaim some values to the world in which these values were unidentified before, but the unconscious quest for them existed. If these values are immanently searched for, transcendent values of the unique Christian faith might emerge and meet the public desire for morality and peace. The ethics of embrace again is the perfect candidate. It responds to the basic human need, promotes flourishing, and represents the real ethics of the *testimony.* Human flourishing—the life worth living—has no meaning without the peace and harmony for which humankind was originally designed. The

---

17. See Theology of Joy Project, http://faith.yale.edu/joy/about.

18 Dávila, "The Gift We Bring," 767.

19 Wolterstorff, "Miroslav Volf On Living One's Faith," 726.

result is being embraced by God and willingly embracing God, myself and my neighbor, including the enemy. In order to convince the world that it needs this peace and harmony of embrace, apologetic bridges need to be built. Those who follow Christ must always bear witness that when the power of love replaces the love for power the world might see some peace.

The apologetic bridge that Volf has chosen is the exploration of the *meaning of life* and *life worth living*. These are philosophical quests that can be used in sharing values of religious experience. Volf rightly recognizes that we are mostly not conscious of the deeper realities of life.[20] We live by the *immediate* reality; there is *no deeper sense*. Unfortunately, if what I do or have is all that I do and all that I have, I have become too small. I have to be greater than what I do. If I am greater than that I can live a life of freedom from greed and other vices, Volf reminds us.[21] To search for the deeper sense is to search for the deeper value of human existence. The deeper value always transcends what I am now or what I have now. Volf's contemporary discussion on public faith, therefore, involves the question of life worth living.

Life Worth Living

My life was empty of meaning until the age of seventeen or eighteen. I was reading poetry, philosophy, humanities, and religious books, but the spiritual darkness I experienced was thick. I gave my best to overcome my existential despair (*angst*) but nothing really worked. My life seemed to have become disposable and not worth anything. Neither Plato nor Nietzsche, neither Shakespeare nor Dostoevsky, could satisfy the thirst of my soul for transcendent permanent meaning. In fact, I tried to follow Nietzsche's principle, captured here by Hergenhahn:

> Meaning and morality of one's life come from within oneself. Healthy, strong individuals seek self expansion by experimenting and by living dangerously. Life consists of an almost infinite number of possibilities and the healthy person explores as many of them as possible. Religions that teach pity, humility, submissiveness, self-contempt, self-restraint, guilt, or a sense of community

20. Volf, "21st Century Thoughts."
21. Ibid.

are simply incorrect. . . . The good life is ever changing, challenging, devoid of regret, intense, creative, and risky.[22]

But my search for Nietzschean intensity and creativity just did not
work. I asked myself a hundred times, Why is this life worth living? and I
could not find a satisfactory answer. What is the meaning of this endless
search for the meaning of life? Unlike Sisyphus, I made a decision to quit
"pushing the stone" when suddenly I received external strength to open
myself to transcendence. The phenomenological gift of light from above
enabled me to open myself and to respond positively to the call for transcendence. By virtue of being light it produced a vibrant and fresh desire
to live and search for ultimate meaning. Transcendence is a gift and a gift
has to be received. Receiving the gift provided the space to find the ultimate
meaning and to live out this meaning in everyday life.

As I was reading Yale Daily News, an article about mental health
caught my attention. The university seems to be concerned with mental
health and wants to reinforce some policies and regulations on withdraw-
als and readmissions of University students.[23] There is no mental health
without a healthy quest for ultimate meaning and continuing openness to
transcendence that offers the gifts of comfort and joy. At least in my experience, Nietzsche's demon of self-expansion has become unwelcome and has
finally been exorcised. This was the work of God!

Why are we often so caught up in the mundane, ordinary, daily rou-
tine of our lives that we are not able to open ourselves to transcendence?
What is the main obstacle to receiving the light? Is there any value in life led
only by satisfaction and pleasure? Why do we have to search for meaning
elsewhere? Some of these perennial questions are taken by Miroslav Volf in
a fresh and innovative way.

In his 2013 Yale lectures entitled "Life Worth Living," Miroslav Volf
begins with Socrates' refutation of Calicles' argument for the value of luxury
and intemperance. Socrates undermines the argument by suggesting the idea
of *basic human insatiability*. There is no satisfaction in constant searching
for more *things*. *Thus, human life is emptied of meaning if there is a relentless
search for physical or intellectual pleasure apart from the ultimate meaning
of life*. Volf argues that science cannot offer a satisfactory solution to the
question of what makes life worth living, and that this question is exorcised
from contemporary academia. Science has no questions about meaning, it

22. Hergenhahn, *Introduction to the History of Psychology*, 226.

23 Li, "Students and Administrators Discuss Mental Health Policy," 8.

just interprets the reality. Regrettably, choices about faith and meaningful life have been placed on the same level as choices about what car I should drive. There must be other ways to expand human productivity, beyond just achieving everyday goals—we should reach for something larger. Volf reminds us that great questions of truth, goodness, and the pursuit of beauty are transcendent. Opening ourselves to something larger than ourselves is a prerequisite for a happier life. As a theologian dealing with ideas, Volf claims that by opening himself to larger things he is "loosing himself" and that is the beauty of life. *Self-transcendence—when I go out of myself—leads to the experience of becoming truly myself.*[24] Although this might sound like mystical self-forgetfulness, as a Christian disciple Volf still stays on the firm ground of the self-sacrificing quest for ultimate meaning *in Christ* and for living out this meaning in loving God and loving neighbor.

In his interview "Immersed in the Ordinary," Volf observes that moments of self-reflection are rare. We are dependent on *spaces that are a little bit out of the ordinary* in order to reflect and to project ourselves into the future. Universities and other institutions do not ask questions such as, "What does it mean to lead our lives, and what is the meaning of life?"[25] We leave the goals to each individual but there are only sporadic moments when we search for that in the community. Churches profess to talk about life worth living, but a good deal of church life is only about *instrumental* religion (much as the universities speak about *instrumental* rationality—searching for means to our own ends). We need space to be called back to reflect on the question, What makes life worth living? concludes Volf.[26] To my questions, Why do we need Christianity to resolve the problem of instrumental religion and instrumental rationality? What are the solutions for the striving of Christian academia towards instrumental rationality? Volf replies that some religions do go against instrumental rationality. However, non-instrumental goals are not always cherished. Volf summarizes the discussion by saying that we need debates about the ends (in different religions and humanist philosophies) but we need much more talk about *gift*, which is always non-instrumental and goes beyond achievement.[27]

24. Volf, "Life Worth Living."
25. See Kronman, *Education's End.*
26. Volf, "Immersed into the Ordinary."
27. Ibid.

In his 2013 Regis College Chancellor's Lecture,[28] Volf reported that at the beginning of American history questions of meaning and life worth living were present. Important existential questions were addressed even by the presidents, who would give lectures on the meaning of life. This changed. The humanities adjusted their methodology in order to have a scientific reputation, and in that process what was most important in humanities has been lost. What is lost is room for conversation with the great thinkers of the past. Plato, for example, has ended up more and more as just a historical figure who is not relevant today. Much of today's humanities supports the idea that there is no human life to be contemplated and that we cannot explore what it means to flourish as human beings. Volf rightly noted that *in contemporary culture we have more or less reduced the question of what makes life worth living to a matter of preference.* Preference, however, belongs to consumerist culture. Pursuing instrumental rationality, universities devolve to research institutes and vocational training. We blindly follow our preferences, seeking to satisfy our desires without exploring what is genuinely desirable. Shaping the desire is what is needed and Christian faith offers the plausible solution: loving God and neighbor. *Christian faith may restore this question for humanity.* If universities do not reflect on what makes life worth living we will not be able to engage in public conversations of that kind, warns Volf.[29]

Again Miroslav Volf is trying to build apologetic bridges between those who have immersed themselves in the ordinary and those who have received the gift of non-instrumental transcendent light. But where is the place of God in a Christian academic environment like Yale?

For some Christians, especially for some college students even at Yale Divinity School, God is portrayed as a heavenly butler, says Volf the theologian—God is here as a benevolent being at the service of our desires. We get harmed and bruised and we need healing and the redemptive touch of Christ that we may continue what we have started. This is all about *our* goals and God's service to those goals; this is the *functionalizing* of religion.[30]

The bottom line of all of this is what Volf expresses in the following statement: *We are losing the sense of genuine transcendence and ability to live*

28. Volf, "Life Worth Living."
29. Ibid.
30. Ibid.

authentic faith, and for that faith to contribute to revival and rejuvenation of our universities.[31]

In practice Volf is trying to live his theology and implement his essential ideas. Therefore, at Yale Divinity School he has developed a course called Life Worth Living. Students read the texts of Moses, Jesus, Buddha, Muhammad, J.S. Mill and Nietzsche to answer questions such as: What is the meaning of leading life according to the texts? What motivations do they offer for a vision of life worth living? What happens when one fails, and what is the remedy?

In his search for transcendence, therefore, Volf also cultivates the culture of inclusiveness and the culture of sharing religious wisdom. Life worth living is the goal but it can be lived only through openness to genuine transcendence, an ability given to *every* human being, not just Christians and Christian academia. Though he is a Christian theologian, Volf is making an effort, by this inclusiveness and openness, to attract non-Christian religious people to the search for transcendence even through Christian means, and to teach Christians that wisdom from any other source is welcome if it strives toward the light. Volf notes in clarification that if God is the Creator of all that is seen and unseen, then all light is God's light, and all truth is God's truth; and if God created and will consummate the world through Christ, the Christ is the Wisdom in all wisdom.[32] I also believe that his project of life worth living is not just another metaphysical theory. It is a genuine attempt to go back to the original and common source of religions.

We shift gears now to talk about the nature and purpose of religion in the context of pursuing life worth living. In his 2013 lecture *Life Worth Living* and in *Flourishing*, Volf makes a distinction between *primary* and *secondary* religions.[33] Primary religions are local, and are concerned with ordinary human flourishing, health, wealth, fertility and longevity. They link the social and the religious (e.g., God bless USA). This becomes an example of a universal religion acting as if it were local and therefore betraying itself.[34] Obviously they lack universality and transcendence. Secondary religions make universal claims about what is just, true, and good for *all* human beings. Secondary religions can flourish even if they fail to have

---

31. Ibid.

32. Volf, to author, May 2015.

33. *Flourishing*, 67.

34. Volf's comments; *Flourishing*.

mundane values. Religion becomes a *distinct* culture system.[35] What is the responsibility of this type of universalistic religion?

> Monotheism and other universalistic religions (namely second-ary) affirm that the individual has the responsibility for leading his own life. They are universalistic because they are not related to specific culture, but they are valid in every culture and speak to every individual. If I believe that my faith supposes this life responsibility, then I have to accept that others have this same re-sponsibility. . . . My faith asks from the other to make decisions of its future. Affirmation of pluralism is in the essence of universalis-tic monotheistic religions. This seems paradoxical but it is true.[36]

I suggest that there is an infinite value in the *ethics of embrace* which has to become the universal part of this prophetic faith. Volf presumably has this principle in mind but it is not explicitly mentioned, perhaps because in *Public Faith* Volf broadens the solutions for human alienation. The ethics of embrace brings love, hope and new orientation to the disillusioned world of estrangement and violence, where peace studies and peace efforts have become more and more useless. Prophetic faith cannot be expressed in ir-relevant or alien language or in purely philosophical terms. The ethics of embrace represents the ultimate theoretical and practical framework which can certainly instigate the desire for non-instrumental human flourishing and life worth living. Everyone, including the most violent perpetrator, likes to *be embraced again*. Every human being strives for both intelligible and practical solutions for the alienation and animosities of this world. Furthermore, the experience of embrace welcomes us into this universe that belongs to the God of embrace. When we feel welcome we feel pro-tected and life is meaningful. The experiential satisfaction of flourishing may come only through realization of the giving and forgiving God who prompts us to give and forgive others. The ascent to God (loving God be-cause he first loved us) and the return to the world (loving neighbor) are both essential for the proper functioning of public faith. *Life worth living is not just a result of a philosophical reasoning, spiritual or religious contempla-tion, or an isolated individual experience, but the outcome of a commitment*

35. In this same context, asked about the relationship between Christ and culture, Volf affirms that there are no pure types. Throughout history there is no single way to relate to the culture (it is too complex). Resistance, affirmation, celebration are different Christian relations to culture.

36 Volf, Interview with B. Sarcevic.

to a deep search for peace and embrace within different forms of the human community. Life worth living is communal.

If the Christian community, according to Miroslav Volf, is "just one of many players, so that from whatever place they find themselves—on the margins, at the center, and anywhere in between—they can promote human flourishing and the common good,"[37] there must be a clear articulation by universalistic religions of what that common good is. Of course, the Christian faith is one of many. We live in a world of particular universalisms, contending with one another and sometimes clashing, and each claiming to be universal. Each should have space to proclaim its own message, as Christians need space to proclaim the message of Christ. The common good is the result of this endeavor. I suggest that the highest expression of this common good is the understanding and implementation of the ethics of embrace. The distance between human beings only reinforces the dark and meaningless quest for self-gratification and self-fulfillment, in which there is no exit from the Nietzschean labyrinth of "possibilities." Coming close will quicken our awareness of the gift of the other, given by the ultimate Other, offering new meaning for our lives. Marriages, families, religions and nations are all possible candidates for receiving the freedom to embrace the other. The communal life of embrace is the practical living out of the intellectual and moral quest for transcendence and life worth living.

Peace Between Religions and the Ethics of Embrace

Sharing the love of Christ with believers of different persuasions is much more important than any theoretical apologetic debate. It took some time for me to come to the realization of this fundamental postulate of the ethics of embrace.

Around the year 2000 I was invited to preach in Macedonia at one of the Christian conventions. I was invited by the members of one of the central churches in Skopje. At my arrival my brothers put me in a gated apartment in the courtyard of the church. That morning I went out of the apartment to take some fresh air and I noticed that the Christian compound was surrounded with many mosques. I had been told that I was fully protected. I had no idea that I would learn an important lesson on the ethics of embrace that day. Suddenly, a man approached the gate. Though I wanted to talk with him outside the courtyard I could not go out because

37. Volf, *A Public Faith*, 79.

I was locked inside the compound. And believe me, I felt somehow happy for that. Though I did not believe in stereotyping religions I still felt comfortable on this side of the gate. The man presented himself as a Muslim believer and was breathing heavily. I asked him about his problem and he explained that he had kidney failure. We started a conversation about the holiness of our sacred books, the Bible and the Quran, and about the role of Muhammad. I pointed to some inconsistences in the Quran, which claims that the Ingil (Gospel) is the Word of God and at the same time affirms that Isa (Jesus) is *not* the Son of God thus denying its own testimony. Interrupting this theological debate, for I knew that it would lead nowhere except controversy and strife, I asked him a simple question: "Would you like me to pray to Allah in the name of Isa for your healing?" He started to shout, "No, not in the name of Isa. Muhammad is great." "Well," I told him, "you tried so many times to pray with that name, perhaps we can now try something different." Sometimes, pragmatic approach to religion is not bad after all. The flourishing principle overshadows theological obscurity. Reluctantly, the man accepted and I prayed to Allah for his healing in the name of Isa. I risked the confusion of naming the true God according to religious context, a point Volf mentions.[38] I believed God could heal this man but I was not expecting much. The man did feel better and walked away without breathing problems, thanking God. I could breathe better too. I also thanked God for teaching me the lesson that His embrace of all human beings and our embrace of each other is much more important than any religious debate or theological polemic. As soon as I realized this I felt the inexpressible joy of embracing my new friend from Skopje. And yes, I preached the Word of God with new enthusiasm and energy that night.

I had shared a nugget of wisdom and a prayer with my Muslim friend, wisdom, as Volf puts it, as an "integrated way of life that enables the flourishing,"[39] I had witnessed without imposition, and that became the key of sharing wisdom.[40] I had freely given my testimony in word and deed and it had become a sharing of wisdom.[41] The integrity of the receiver was respected and I did honor the limits of what this man was willing to receive.[42] Finally, this person to whom I gave had become a giver too, and

38. Ibid., 81.
39. Ibid., 101.
40. Ibid., 106.
41. Ibid., 107.
42. Ibid., 109.

I had become a receiver.[43] He taught me to honor and respect the otherness of faith and to be ready to promote human flourishing just by friendly interaction and exchange of our common gifts. Life worth living is the life of embrace of the other. It is the fulfilling life indeed.

What would happen in this corrupt and alienated world if all of us found ways to build bridges of understanding between religions and to embrace those of different religious persuasion by promoting mutual sharing of wisdom, love and tolerance? Isn't the pursuit of life worth living a universal agenda of all the pious?

First of all, according to Miroslav Volf, we should protect other religions from stereotyping by others, and "build bridges between religious cultures." Rather than being indifferent, we need to *promote* it.[44] Sharing wisdom[45] is an ultimate call for every disciple of Christ. From a Christian perspective, as Volf reminds us, this sharing makes sense only if that wisdom is allowed to counter the multiple manifestations of self-absorption by givers and receivers alike and to connect them with what ultimately matters—God, whom we should love with all our being, and neighbors, whom we should love as ourselves.[46]

Religions are irreducibly distinct,[47] so overlooking the differences or promoting secularism as an alternative will not help. The only solution, for Volf, lies in concentration on the *internal resources* of each religion by fostering the culture of peace. For Christianity it means going back to the center and redefining our identity.[48] He writes,

> To speak in a Christian voice is to speak out of these two fundamental convictions: that God loves all people, including the transgressors, and that *religious identity is circumscribed by permeable boundaries.*[49]

In his interview in Croatia in 2001 Volf clearly highlights this point: "Identity is not just what I am, without comparing myself with others; identity's boundaries are permeable. I am not the other, but if I am exposed to

43. Ibid., 111.
44. Volf, *Against the Tide*, 157.
45. Ibid., 108.
46. Volf, *A Public Faith*, 117.
47. Ibid., 130.
48. Ibid., 132.
49. Italics added for emphasis. Ibid., 133.

the other I am living a richer life with the other."[50] Permeable boundaries, therefore, are just the result of my exposure and interaction with those of other religious persuasions. This exposure has become the natural outcome of my fervent desire to love and be loved, to accept and be accepted. Later I will return to this subject.

In his interview *Multiple Faiths, Common Worlds*[51] Volf asks how the market contributes to human flourishing with its overlapping of economic and religious values. If globalization is shaped by a universal notion of human flourishing it is on a collision course with religion, because religions are exclusive. Volf recognizes that in every encounter there are always six images: my image of myself, my image of you, your image of yourself, your image of me, my image of us, and your image of us. All these images need transformation. As religious people we have to affirm the truth of our given way of life, but the affirmation of truth is incompatible with tolerance (at least some faiths believe). Volf believes that it is possible to affirm the truth and yet be tolerant, expressing *beneficence* toward others not just *tolerance*. Nonetheless, we always have partial knowledge of religious consciousness, not absolute or what we claim to be absolute. For that reason we also learn from others and have to make a shift from what is different to what is common. Of course, we should not abandon all interest in what is different. Both are important. Faith starts not with knowledge but with action (common action).[52] This call for common action is one of the key postulates of Volf's theology as a way of life. If the shift towards the commonalities were successfully made, religions would be able to act out their beliefs toward the life worth living and toward mutual embrace.

In his 2014 Payton Lecture "World Faiths: What They Are and Why They Matter" Volf emphasizes that *our Christian articulation must take into account the fact that we are always related to others, and that I have to construe my own perspective taking other perspectives into account.* There are some significant common features in world religions, and from our own Christian perspective it is possible to read other faiths and take notice of the commonalities,.[53] The ideal of democracy has become increasingly

50. Volf, "21st Century Thoughts."

51. Volf, "Multiple Faiths, Common World."

52. Ibid.

53 Volf outlines 6 common features of world religions: 1. Cosmotheistic religions two worlds account of reality, without dualistic they have transcendent and mundane and give primacy to transcendence, 2. People relate to God and spirit as a *community* as a given socio linguistic, world religion create pan human religious community of individuals,

popular, but *what happens when religious people embrace democracy?* The resurgence of faith and the popularity of pluralistic democracy seem to be two opposite realities. However, exclusive religion does not need to become politically exclusive. *This insight is necessary in order to set up a political framework to negotiate differences in a peaceful way.* This is one of Volf's pivotal ideas.

All world religions, explains Volf, have their ordinary accounts of flourishing. They do not just escape ordinary life by attending only to transcendence, but *see themselves as ways of living the ordinary life.* We live ordinary life well when we align purpose with transcendence. We do not live by bread alone. Nicholas Wolterstorff's idea of life being led well (loving God and neighbor) and life going well (healing, feeding, prospering) is well illustrated in the book of Job.[54] Volf uses the story of Job to demonstrate the fact that life can be led well even when it is not going well. However, at the end of this saga God confirms the perennial principle that life led well *leads to* life going well.

Therefore, on the ground of commonalities, all religions should lead conversations which will somehow contribute to the common good of life worth living (life going well) in the social setting. In order to do that, religions and religious identities have to have *permeable boundaries.* Permeable boundaries are indispensable prerequisites for openness in spite of obvious differences and historical alienations. This mutual penetration of some values and experiences into the tradition of the other creates a space for embracing the other and therefore, living a more thriving life. There is no peace and prosperity in self-alienation from others.

What is, after all, Volf's contribution to creating peace among religions? First of all, he promotes *dialogue.* Is this dialogue sincere or a mere formality? In his own experience of dialogue between the Vatican and

---

3. Universal claims unlike local religions, what is just and good for ALL human beings, problem of sin, 4. All have goods beyond ordinary human flourishing (local religions fertility, happiness and premature death) world religions speak about goods that transcend human flourishing, through failing (dying young on the cross) you can flourish too, 5. Distinct cultural systems (local religions and culture are the same), world religions are autonomous systems, distinct, they can transcend all political borders, 6. Local religions are in the mood of ascent, neo pagan faith; This ascent to life gives way to quarrel with life, things are not what they are supposed to be, prophetism, asceticism, transcendence ought to shape mundane reality. All world religions are more than just cosmology and anthropology; they have symbols, rituals etc. World religions are sometimes less than we describe, Christian flag for example, emptied of 6 features. Volf, "World Faiths."

54. Ibid.

Pentecostalism he noticed that some dialogue is based on self-interest and some other dialogue is formal. In spite of human shortcomings and failures dialogue moves things forward. Commenting on Hans Küng's assertion that there is "no peace among peoples without peace among religions" Volf says that it is partially true, but he also claims that today there is much more violence in the living room, though people are of the same religion, than in wars.[55]

According to Volf, peace between religions depends not only on recognition of the *essence of true religion* but even on the premise that one affirms love of God and neighbor (monotheistic religions) and the other does not (as in the case of Buddhism). True religion may be found in the Old Testament Scriptures, and it is always based on justice and love, not on rituals and ceremonies. True religion is loving God and loving neighbor; this is genuine spirituality. Faith is living in us, and we should be in relationship to the source of all meaning. Religions are not about political parties but genuine spiritual experience. In this context peace between religions is possible only if individuals recognize the essence of true religion.[56]

The ethics of embrace, I would add, does confirm the universal love of God, and by embracing the other we may create the space for penetrable boundaries of faith experience. It is, therefore, again the perfect candidate for sharing wisdom in interreligious dialogue and life, and for promoting peace. Indeed, Volf affirms that embrace is the metaphor that expresses better than any other the centered and dynamic nature of identities in relation; it is the prism through which to read his entire theology.[57]

Moreover, according to Volf, interreligious exchange consists of both "reading others' beliefs and practices through the lenses of our own tradition and examining how our own beliefs and practices are read by others and why."[58] Consequently, "we need to resist the lure of pridefully perceiving ourselves as only givers of wisdom, rather than always also its receivers—and receivers from both expected and unexpected sources."[59] This sharing of wisdom should be done in non-aggressive and non-violent ways.[60] As Oswald Chambers wonderfully put it:

55. Volf, "21 Century Thoughts."
56. Ibid.
57. Volf, to author, May 2015.
58. Volf, *Against the Tide*, 122.
59. Ibid., 109.
60. Ibid., 114-16.

It is perilously possible to make our conceptions of God like molten lead poured into a specially designed mould, and when it is cold and hard we fling it at the heads of the religious people who don't agree with us.[61]

On the other hand, we should not zero in on what is the same or zero in on what is different. "Since truth matters, and since a false pluralism of approving pats on the back is cheap and short-lived, we will rejoice over overlaps and engage others over differences and incompatibilities, so as both to learn from and teach others."[62] Thus, if I am reading Volf well, permeable boundaries *do not assume the total loss of the identity* but promote its preservation, enrichment, and expansion within the encounter with the other. Volf indeed confirms this:

> It is important to keep the authenticity of personal conviction. I do not see that there are reasons why we should compromise our standpoint and our authentic conviction in the encounter with others. On the other hand, it is important to distinguish between the essential and the marginal in my convictions. My experience in the encounter with Muslims and others is the following: If I live my faith deeply, that deep living of my faith does not alienate me from the other but brings me closer to them.[63]

In this regard I did ask Dr. Volf, How risky are these permeable boundaries for Christian faith? How can we absorb other values of other religions in this process? His response was unequivocal: Christ is the source of wisdom. We always follow Him at a distance; we cannot fully imitate him because of his unique divine-human nature and his unique redemptive death at the cross as his way of forgiving human beings. There is a risk, and the risk is in setting up *non-permeable* boundaries, when we close ourselves off. Knowledge is always provisional and never absolute. I am always less than I can be. If I closed myself off I would not be able to fulfill my mission, concludes Volf.[64]

Let us turn now to the most challenging religious encounter for Volf today, the one between Christianity and Islam. In his book *Allah* (2011), following a lengthy discussion on the similarities and differences between Islam and Christianity, and ten sacred commandments against extremism,

61. Chambers, *Disciples Indeed*, 388.

62. Volf, *Against the Tide*, 125.

63 Volf, Interview with B. Sarcevic.

64. Volf, Interview by author, July 8, 2014.

injustice, prejudice, disrespect, and exclusivism, Volf summarizes his arguments in the following way:

> The claim that Christians and Muslims, notwithstanding their im-
> portant and ineradicable differences, have a common and similarly
> understood God (1) delegitimizes religious motivation to violence
> between them and (2) supplies motivation to care for others and to
> engage in a vigorous and sustained debate about what constitutes
> the common good in the one world we share.[65]

Volf's goal, in this book, is not so much theological as pragmatic or rather
"social" based on the reality of co-existence, although in encounter with
others the goal might be spiritual and soteriological, because, after all, we
bear witness to faith in Christ as the way to God. But here Volf wishes to
provide the space for non-violent sharing of wisdom or witness and embracing the other as the common good for all. He remains faithful to the
basic paradigm of his multifaceted approach to this problem, namely, ethics of embrace.

In his interview on *Public Faith* he was asked, "Do Muslims and Christians have a set of common fundamental values providing possibilities for
negotiating differences in a peaceful way?" Volf replied in the following way.
If these values are completely different there will be no moral agreements
or even convergences. In fact, there are significant overlapping values. If
we are going to live as responsible citizens in the same political community
with others, we need a set of common values so that engagement may be
productive. The *Allah* book provides this common set of values. If there
are common values, this is what public engagement should look like. The
Egyptian revolution is an example, Volf reminds us. Muslims, Christians
and secularists deposed the dictator, searching for the common good.[66]
According to Volf, this is a very good example of engagement in the public
realm in a pluralistic way. Of course, it is easier to depose a dictator than to
build up a common future. Yet, this should be possible in a Muslim cultural
environment, concludes Volf.[67]

In his early phase lecture "Do Muslims and Christians believe in
the same God?" Volf spoke about dogmatic similarities and differences

---

65. Volf, *Allah*, 262.

66. There are, of course, many different interpretations of the causes of "Arab
spring," but my emphasis is contextual.

67. Volf, "Public Faith."

between Islam and Christianity, and presented some significant ideas. He presented four basic features:

1. Both Christians and Muslims believe in the categorical difference of God—there is no other object who is categorically different from creation, though we use different names for God.

2. Muslims more and more have started to acknowledge that Christians believe in the *unity* of God, *one* essence numerically. This seems like a common ground.

3. One God, love God, love neighbor, mercy, and compassion are the basic commonalities of these religions.

4. The worship of Muslims might be explained as: partly rightly worship partly known God (suggestion for Muslims). Other alternatives are rightly worship the true God and fully known God [heavenly ideal], rightly worship the false god (not clear what this might be but it is not Kierkagaard's legacy).

I asked a question about the commonalities between Islam and Christianity: What about the risk of creating "Chrislam?"[68] Volf clearly indicates that he does not support fusion of religions, because he believes in the unique revelation of God incarnate in Christ. Volf believes that some pastors and theologians who accused him of creating "Chrislam" did not comprehend the purpose of his *Allah* book and other materials. Relations between Islam and Christianity are not only about salvation of the soul. Do Muslim values go against Christ? The goods of life are not only about salvation. Volf's purpose is to point to the possibilities of co-existence in this world, both communities mutually witnessing and engaging publicly.[69] As I have already mentioned, Volf's purpose is not primarily soteriological or theological, but pragmatic or social.

Although Volf's intention is to speak primarily about reconciliation processes and not matters of salvation or dogmatic theology, he does deal with political and moral theology, and in fact finds it necessary to address critical doctrinal issues in the conversation with Islam—for example, the Trinity. Here I have no space or intention to deal with extensive debates, but Volf clearly argues that both Muslims and Christians worship God in his *oneness* and that, in spite of accusations, Christians *are* true monotheists.

68. Volf, Interview by author, July 8, 2014.
69. Ibid.

He was engaging in dialogue with Muslim scholars even before the publication in 2008 of Archbishop of Canterbury Rowan Williams' expression of one God existing "in a threefold pattern of interdependent action."[70] Volf, therefore, always takes a Christian stand and is careful to preserve orthodox Christian formulations. Nevertheless, this is not the primary purpose of his book *Allah* or any other of Volf's work on this topic. Absence of violence and care for others is what he is interested in, and these are possible only if we open ourselves and create a possibility for others to enter our space and be embraced. I remember with pleasure Professor Philippe Capelle from the Catholic Institute in Paris who opened his personal and professional space to work with me as an evangelical philosopher and theologian. Our common sharing of wisdom contributed to the development of my post-doctoral project about the sense of divinity.[71] Within the permeable boundaries of our identities something good always results from our promotion of the ethics of embrace. As we listen and learn from others we grow in the grace of mutual understanding and enrichment that leads to life worth living.

Nevertheless, this sharing of common space and identity is not and should not become a *fusion of horizons* or the creation of an artificial all-inclusive super-religion where anything goes and everything is validated. Paris, France, 2007. As an evangelical Adventist minister with a Free Church background, I was invited to participate in a common prayer service for peace. That was a kind of annual ecumenical endeavor in the Catholic church of St Peter and Paul. I did not feel comfortable to participate in this common worship service in the cathedral, not because I could not open myself and create a space in sharing religious wisdom but simply because I did not believe in the fusion of beliefs and liturgical practices that seemed to be required in order to come to that sharing. I do not believe Volf has in mind this fusion when he speaks about permeable boundaries. He can pray with Muslims while acknowledging differences, and he can participate without compromise in devotional services with those who believe in the self-revelation of God in Christ.[72] But my experience in Paris, even though it did not include any coerciveness, stimulated

70. Volf refers to Dr. Williams' letter in his article, "Allah and the Trinity," 20–24. There is a link to Dr. Williams' letter at http://rowanwilliams.archbishopofcanterbury. org/articles.php/1107/a-common-word-for-the-common-good.

71. Santrac, *Comparison of John Calvin and Alvin Plantinga's Concept of Sensus Divinitatis*.

72. Volf, to author, May 2015.

me to think that the absorption of all differences in one conglomerate of beliefs might constitute a denial of the ethics of embrace and the principle of sharing wisdom. Recent developments (2014) in ecumenical reconciliation between Pope Francis and charismatic Christians, including some evangelical Christians, create more challenges to the same reality.[73] If we do not properly define certain boundaries in beliefs we will lose the variety and richness of Christian traditions in an ecumenical quandary in which there is no dialogue or sharing, and in which *fusion* of horizons becomes only *confusion*. The boundaries that are "permeable" should be those of self-dependence, self-aggrandizement, pride in the uniqueness and rigidity of our tradition, exclusion of others based on one's preference for one way and one method, prejudice, hatred, bigotry and exclusivism, but not the boundaries of conscience-driven foundational beliefs based on honest and open searching for God in his Word. Reconciliation as a religious project could be in danger of becoming only a political agenda that finally does violence to the inner convictions and personal freedom of a believer. Reconciliation must be based on the totally free willingness to enter the space of each other without sacrificing, but promoting, what is most sacred in our religious convictions. Reconciliation that is compulsory robs us of joy and the delight of freely embracing the other—the transcendent joy and delight my Muslim friend and I felt in Skopje, Macedonia.

73. See Armstrong, "Bishop Tony Palmer and Pope Francis."

5

FAITH AND GLOBALIZATION

THE MOST RECENT WORK of Miroslav Volf centers on the dynamic relationship between world religions and the reality of globalization. At the Center for Faith and Culture at Yale Divinity School I was privileged to participate in the discussion group dealing with the manuscript called *Faith and Globalization*, which Dr. Volf submitted to us. This is now the book titled *Flourishing: Why We Need Religion in a Globalized World*, recently (2015) released by Yale University Press. Based on my observations I have chosen a few elements of the work that may be the most significant for understanding the relation between faiths and the globalizing processes. Juxtaposition between Volf's paradigm of life worth living and ethics of embrace is again evident in this project.

In the prologue Volf clearly indicates that the concept of globalization is not after all so foreign to world religions. He claims:

> The world religions are part of the dynamics of globalization—they are, in a sense, the original globalizers and still remain among the drivers of globalization processes—and globalization is part of the dynamics of religions, their moral and doctrinal self-articulations, their cultural and political formations, and their intergenerational and missionary dissemination. Globalization is *within* religions and world religions are *within* globalization.[1]

For Volf, universal *global* world religions provide the idea of *transcendence* that leads to a vision of human flourishing that is part of the global

---

1 Volf, *Flourishing*, 1-2.

vision of this world.[2] World religions (especially Christian faith)[3] serve as catalysts of the globalizing process in such a way that they assess and evaluate what is life worth living.[4] Life worth living cannot be based only on the search for daily bread, for bread alone is not the basis of our human existence. Volf unambiguously accentuates his main point:

> My main thesis is simple. I can state it in the words that, according to the Hebrew Bible, Moses said to the children of Israel at the end of forty years of wandering in the wilderness and the words that Jesus, weakened after forty days of fasting in the wilderness, hurled at the Tempter in self-defense (Deuteronomy 8:3; Matthew 4:4): "One does not live by bread alone, but by every word that comes from the mouth of the Lord." The greatest of all temptations isn't to serve false gods, as monotheists like to think. The greatest of all temptations, equally hard to resist in abundance and in want, is to believe and act as if human beings lived by bread alone, as if their entire lives should revolve around the creation, improvement, and distribution of worldly goods. Serving false gods—or turning the one true God into a mere bread provider, which amounts to the same thing—is the consequence of succumbing to this grand temptation.[5]

The great temptation to which world religions frequently succumb, therefore, is to devolve either into mere instruments of procuring bread or into weapons in mundane struggles over bread.[6]

In fact, in order to avoid this basic temptation both globalization processes and world religions somehow need to contribute to "improving the state of the world." There is a mutual shaping, which must be done in such a way that its effects are judged positively in moral terms. Globalization processes need to become more open to the religious vision of moral frameworks and life worth living, and religions need to become more responsive to one another as they articulate a common vision of human flourishing and become "shapers" of globalization.[7] This is the main challenge by

2. Ibid.

3. Volf's standpoint is primarily Christian. He argues that his agenda is to draw the attention of other world religions to the common project of life worth living as an assessment of globalizing processes. Ibid., 21.

4. Ibid., 16-17.

5. Ibid., 21-22.

6. Ibid.

7. Ibid., 26.

which the whole project of globalization stands or falls. Volf recognizes the complexity of this task.[8] Only if world religions find common ground in expressing and articulating their *common affirmation of transcendence* and its relationship to the vision of human flourishing[9] will they be able to shape the globalization process. Several times in our discussion on his book at Yale, Volf clearly confirmed the importance of this overarching vision of life worth living that might steer the globalization ship. I will come back to this most critical issue later.

For Volf, the main problem or contention lies in the discrepancy between the vision of life worth living offered by market-driven globalization (shaped only by interest in the mundane) and the vision of life worth living offered by religions that introduce the element of transcendence which cannot be overlooked.[10] "We need to rescue globalization from these destructive propensities and place it at the service of humanity," stresses Volf.[11] Using the legacy of both John Paul II and the Dalai Lama he concludes:

> Globalization needs to be shaped so it can help make the lives of all human beings go well, and provide them with what is needed to lead healthy, creative, and long lives. More important, globalization needs to be tamed so it will be less likely to rob us of our humanity by making our moral lives subservient to our material wants, whether these are very basic (like three simple meals a day) or highly exclusive (like a space tourism excursion).[12]

Both exclusive humanists and religionists get it wrong, Volf recognizes. We will get nowhere by emphasizing all the hindrances of religion or by supporting the indispensable role of religion in society.[13] Only the prophetic impulse of religion, based on promotion of life worth living (life led well and going well)[14] and propelled by democratic processes,[15] can shape the

---

8. The difficulty lies in the "taming globalization itself." Ibid., 58.

9. "Reference to transcendence isn't an *add-on* to humanity; rather, it defines human beings. That's the structural restlessness of human hearts." Ibid., 82.

10. Ibid., 23-24. I believe Volf would agree that market-driven globalization operates with a notion of human flourishing that is in important ways closer to the notion of human flourishing in primary religions than in secondary ones.

11. Ibid., 47.

12. Ibid., 49.

13. Ibid., 50-51.

14. Ibid., 75.

15. Ibid., 65.

course of globalization. The process of globalization, on the other hand, is an ally of religions[16] because

> It is helping religions free themselves from the false alternatives of either being personal but publicly inconsequential or publicly significant but politically authoritarian. It is strengthening the possibility for religions to be personally appropriated, publicly engaged, and politically pluralistic all at the same time.[17]

In Chapter 3 of *Flourishing* Volf introduces the topic of religious freedom. He claims that "a world religion that curtails the freedom of religion is in deep tension with itself, and it may even be self-contradictory."[18] World religions, publicly engaged, have to stay away from the temptation of excluding others from the public realm or pushing them back into privacy and exclusion. Legitimate respect for all needs to be reconciled with the transcendent claims of religions.[19] Volf calls for complete freedom of religion, impartiality of the state and an equal voice for all; this leads us to the idea that religious exclusivists could and should embrace political pluralism.[20] Volf's main point, expanded in Chapter 4, therefore, becomes the following. Adherents of exclusivism have embraced political pluralism in the past—indeed, religious exclusivists first articulated the idea of political pluralism—many of them embrace it today, and there is no good reason to think that they will not be able to do so in the future. On the contrary: some of their foundational religious convictions favor political pluralism and in a globalized world of intermingled religious communities they will have a strong motivation to embrace political pluralism. This major point in the book is furthermore sustained by various historical and theological arguments.[21] Volf argues that religious exclusivists, if they live according to ideals promoting the common good and human flourishing, and if they do not "succumb to the culture of the managed pursuit of pleasure," and if

16. Ibid., 90.

17. Ibid., 87.

18. Ibid., 115.

19. Ibid., 133.

20. Ibid., 134-35. "Clearly, it is not only adherents of world religions who need to be persuaded to embrace this version of political pluralism. Many nonreligious people aren't convinced either. A major reason for skepticism is the observation that most adherents of world religions are religious exclusivists coupled with the conviction that the affirmation of religious exclusivism is deeply incongruous with endorsement of pluralism as a political project." Ibid., 135-36.

21. Ibid., 144; 159-60.

they paradoxically strengthen their basic convictions by engaging in social issues, will be able to embrace political pluralism and become allies of the globalization process, even though they may be its sharpest critics.[22] Obviously, Volf struggles here with all fundamentalist religious movements that hardly fit the picture of modern democracy and pluralistic globalization. Volf has a real concern over these 'betrayers' of globalization. Nonetheless, if they make a shift in their vision of transcendence and properly relate it to the mundane, there is a hope that they can make a significant contribution to the common good as well.

In the last chapter of *Flourishing* Volf reminds us again that we "are thrown into a mesh of interdependence" and have to learn how to live together and how to seek reconciliation if conflict arises.[23] The ambiguous globalizing processes[24] prompt us to explore new ways of common life and search for realities that will bring peace.

Volf again insists that the metaphor of *embracing* is appropriate for describing reconciliation processes in the global community. Awareness of being in the global community, acceptance of different identities, living the principle of reciprocity,[25] and being willing to have permeable boundaries all represent different facets of the *embracing* experience.[26] Some productive clashes[27] might lead to recognition of the necessity for at least some version of the Golden Rule,[28] which is, in fact, embedded in every world religion in different ways. Volf argues:

> Without loss to religion's integrity, these motifs can be highlighted and reshaped so as to make it possible for religions practiced thickly as ways of life to coexist peacefully under the same roof and negotiate their differences in a vigorous and yet productive way.[29]

Therefore, as I argued above and highlight again here, Volf's ideal of reshaping the globalizing processes by the world religions' common vision of life worth living has to be grounded again in the indispensable

22. Ibid., 160.

23. Ibid., 174.

24. Ibid., 181-82.

25. "Whatever rights and privileges they want to claim for themselves, they must grant the same to all others." Ibid., 192.

26. Ibid., 182.

27. Ibid., 192.

28. Ibid., 192-93.

29. Ibid., 193.

ethics of embrace. The value of life worth living and flourishing in a general sense is always dependent on the willingness of the global community to recognize the need for acceptance and favorable reception of the other in the act of *embrace.*

Is Volf then asking that the world religions search for a common articulation of a common transcendent vision, which then could be practically implemented by all religions in a common pragmatic reshaping of the globalizing processes? Volf is adamant that he is not advocating such. While all religions place stress on the primacy of transcendence, their formal features make it possible for them to jointly affirm procedures of engagement (such as respect for freedom, equality, etc.) and therefore engage in productive debates at religious, cultural and political levels. Agreement, disagreement or compromise may occur on all these levels.[30]

Volf, therefore, rejects the proposal of a "world theology" based on a unified and universal vision which may articulate a common religious core for the benefit of humanity,[31] but he suggests an alternative:

> Even though world religions have distinct metaphysical frameworks, readily distinguishable accounts of life worth living, and differing notions of the human predicament and of salvation,[32] they have . . . structural affinities and, equally important, they share some basic principles that guide human interaction, such as the commitment to truthfulness, justice, and compassion as well as the conviction that ethical norms apply universally, to coreligionists and outsiders . . . *Overlaps among world religions in convictions yield nothing like "the world theology" or "the global worldview," but these religions' common convictions can underpin a set of global rules and commitments necessary for global order, civility, and the pursuit of common good. Within such a global order, adherents of world religions can be assertive in promoting their visions of human flourishing and yet live in peace with one another and with a-religious people.* Religions would then "compete with one another," not only in "good works," as the famous verse in the Qur'an puts it (5:48), but also in visions of the good life. They would then be able both to enrich each other and to help shape globalization (italics mine).[33]

30. Volf, to author, May 2015.

31. Ibid., 91–92.

32. See Heim, *Salvations.*

33. Volf, *Flourishing*, 92–93.

Thank you, Dr. Volf, for this insightful and brilliant proposal for making all religions relevant and dynamic in the globalized society today, that they may become shapers of globalization. There might be, however, at least two doubts about the final success of this project. Christian faith does not need to impose on other religions its transcendent vision and ethical commitment as the most plausible. The Christian vision does not endorse a global rule. Volf clearly maintains that religions do not need to believe the same about God to agree on the moral level—God's grace is at work even where God is not rightly recognized or even where he is not worshipped at all. [34] Nevertheless, I believe there has to be a *minimum of common knowledge and experience of transcendence* in order to express its implications properly as a moral vision or practice.

This leads me to my second doubt. Beyond negating the necessity for one globalized world religion and beyond calling all world religions to accomplish the task of articulating their own visions of life worth living,[35] Volf also calls for the establishment of global rules based on common moral convictions leading to global *order*. In this common space religions would become more assertive in promoting their visions of life worth living and taming the processes of globalization. The language of "global rules" or "global order" implies that religious and ethical boundaries would be transcended. Does this mean that individual religious convictions and expressions of these would be overruled? Volf adamantly says no: pluralistic structures, imperfect as they are, would allow each person and each community to live as they see fit, and in peace, within a common space.[36] Volf confirmed in an interview with me that the most basic temptation of every religion is to align itself with the state power.[37] His vision disallows the creation of some kind of coalition between religions and governments. If religions need global order so as to be more assertive and to promote

---

34. Volf, to author, May 2015.

35. Volf, "Blessing or Curse?"

36. Volf, to author, May 2015.

37. I asked, "Why is globalization helpful in the relationship between church and state and not welcome in the relationship between faith and the market/economy?" Volf answered, "When religions align themselves with politics they become servants of politics and support political violence. Faith distinct from politics must be the fundamental stance. God is more to be obeyed than human beings. Globalization pluralizes the spaces, and no one has the right to unify people under one religion—this is a totalitarian temptation. Secularization of religion (by alignment with the state) leads to true loss of transcendence." Volf, Interview by author, July 14, 2014.

life worth living, then they have to lean on power *beyond themselves*—the power of a political pluralism that is at all times sensitive to the understandings and needs of different religions. This power would need at least to play the role of the guarantor of successful implementation of global moral rules and preservation of the global moral order within which every religion will have time and space to express its vision of human flourishing. If this power is a-religious (that is, exclusively humanist) it will not be sensitive enough to the different needs of world religions and will probably oppress people of faith; if it is religious (religionist) it will diminish the space for the expression of a-religious people, and finally, if it is Christian it might have to play the inquisitive authoritarian role which contradicts both religious freedom and Christian mission in its core essence. Therefore, I believe that the project of attaining a *common* moral articulation of world religions by rule and order in the process of globalization is implausible and even impossible.

I am of the conviction that world religions should not strive to articulate a common moral vision or create a common global order with the assistance of some person or organization who would ensure that peaceful dialogue is promoted, but they should strive to work out their own distinctive moral visions with respect for all, as is necessary in pluralistic liberal democracy and the complexity of globalizing processes. True love is in no need of power. The temptation of universalism is always to gain power. The power of love should replace the love for power in every sense. The power of Christian faith, for example, to tame and shape globalization does not reside in its ability to provide universal global moral rules or to impose a universal moral order on the process of globalization, but paradoxically and authentically to live counter-globalized and sometimes even counter-religious prophetic faith as a public testimony, resisting the temptations of both withdrawal and coerciveness. In this ambiguous life-worth-living journey the cross of Christ cannot and should not be avoided or compromised but fully *embraced*. If it is not intrinsically good, the cross at least leads to life worth living. Taming what Marine Le Pen calls the "barbaric beast" of globalization[38] might after all be a dangerous mission, though I do agree with Volf that the sins of nationalism at the political level are sometimes worse than the sins of globalization at the economic level. "The plague of the spirit of this religious age"[39] might cause insensitivity to the

---

38 Le Pen, "Globalization is Barbarous."

39. Jesus answered, "My kingdom is not of this world" (John 18:36). "The great enemy of the Lord Jesus Christ today is the idea of practical work that has no basis in the New

essential experience of Christian faith based on a proper relationship with its Founder. The identity that could be lost is not the identity of core beliefs or moral convictions and boundaries, or even the identity of a Christian church as such, but the identity of cross-centered and cross-oriented disciples. The common transcendent vision that leads to ethical commitment with the purpose of providing space for embrace must, for Christian faith, always be founded on the cross, the self-sacrificial love principle, and there is a slight chance that world religions would agree on this point. If you ask me, and I am sure that Volf would agree, believers, Christian or not, who follow this principle are the real promoters of peace between religions, of the common vision of transcendence that leads to life worth living and of the ethics of embrace; they are the true shapers and tamers of market-driven and power-driven globalization. But there might be a Bonhofferian price to be paid. "My kingdom is not of this world," says Christ,[40] even if the religions are competing in good works.

Peace Between Nations and the Ethics of Embrace

> Christians must organize demonstrations, the leaders of its churches must make public statements, and individuals must begin collecting signatures—all to prevent the leaders of our nation from engaging in an immoral and unwise war.[41]

The students in my *Christian Ethics in Modern Society* class are always perplexed when we come to realize that the Sermon on the Mount works only for the individual but not for communities and nations. The ethics of war seem incompatible with the admonition of Jesus to turn the other cheek

---

Testament but comes from the systems of the world. This work insists upon endless energy and activities, but no private life with God. The emphasis is put on the wrong thing. Jesus said, 'The kingdom of God does not come with observation . . . For indeed, the kingdom of God is within you' (Luke 17:20-21). It is a hidden, obscure thing. An active Christian worker too often lives to be seen by others, while it is the innermost, personal area that reveals the power of a person's life. We must get rid of the plague of the spirit of this religious age in which we live. In our Lord's life there was none of the pressure and the rushing of tremendous activity that we regard so highly today, and a disciple is to be like his Master. The central point of the kingdom of Jesus Christ is a personal relationship with Him, not public usefulness to others." Oswald Chambers,"Unheeded Secret."

40. John 18:36.

41. Volf, *Against the Tide*, 154.

to your enemy or abuser. The "politics" of Jesus[42] seem to be irreconcilable with a noble patriotic desire to defend our identity and our fatherland.

How functional is the counter-politics of Jesus, the politics of giving and forgiving based on the ethics of embrace in a world full of strife, violence and wars that are often justifiable and validated by common sense? Evidently, the re-emergence of the Cold War today, as one example, has awakened some Christians and secularists to renew the quest for the ultimate solution of this perennial problem. Does Miroslav Volf have a satisfactory answer to this question? I am not certain about his position on ethics of war, but I am sure we can learn a lot about reconciliatory processes from his insights.

Volf is convinced that the most violent places are living rooms, not battle fields.[43] He has said this more than once, and it is a profound observation. Everything starts with the most intimate relationships and family ties. Frustrated and unfulfilled spouses, parents or children are major causes of much strife in this alienated world. Furthermore, when communities, ethnic groups or nations are pushed closer together, continues Volf in the same interview, the result is a *proximity tension*. The only solution for this continuing pressure of animosity between parties that through historical necessity have to live together is the power of *reconciliation*, the power of *love* as active care towards the different one, towards the other. Of course, we do not need to be the same to live together, we need divine hope to be able to live together in spite of our differences, concludes Volf.[44] Volf is noted, therefore, for his insistence on acceptance, forgiveness and reconciliation between nations or ethnic groups that for historical reasons have to live in proximity. His perseverance in this call amazes us, since we are witnesses of so many different failures in this area.

In the interview *Public Faith*, Volf clearly contends that political liberalism as currently conceived and practiced has serious problems. It seems that we have not found an alternative to living under the same roof. "*We need faith-friendly democracies and we need democracy-friendly faith,*"[45] exclaims Volf. According to this faith-based theory we should abandon secular versions of political liberalism and allow religious factors to insert themselves into the political realm. When I engage in political activities

42. Yoder, *The Politics of Jesus.*

43. Volf, Evangelical Alliance Interview.

44. Ibid.

45. Volf, "Public Faith."

I ought not to leave my faith behind, explains Volf. Social activism is the result of my public faith. However, religious *totalitarianism*, like the Muslim Brotherhood in Egypt, tends to take over the public realm and impose itself as the *dominant* system. Christians are not immune to this disease. In order to avoid both secularism and the saturation of religion in the public realm, Volf proposes that all faiths should engage with one another and search for the common good by treating others as they would like to be treated. This seems a necessary condition for genuine peace between nations or ethnic or religious groups. Volf is consistently devoted to his overarching vision of reconciliation between nations and peace in the world through the renewal or revival of the original purpose of each world religion, through active engagement in the public realm, and through treating others with love and respect. Secularism, idle faith and coercive faith have obviously failed in this regard.

In his interview in Croatia in 2001 Volf spoke about some important roots of the problem in this divided world. Roots of animosity always remain because of the *desire for pure identity* and the *will to power*. Exclusion based on pure identity and the will to power instead of the will to embrace will destroy modern civilizations as they have destroyed civilizations in the past. Volf also mentions material causes as very important. Where valuable resources are in the hands of a minority, pressure will be created, and conflict will be inevitable. There is no one, continues Volf, who rules the process that we may talk with him and find a solution. Auto-processes of independent systems rule, and we need to confront them. We cannot stay isolated, concludes Volf, with prophetic conviction.[46] How should we insert the values of the common good based on religious sentiment into this space of auto-processes and independent systems? There is no final solution, but we should certainly avoid some extremes.

Self-isolation of Christians is indeed hazardous both for Christians and for this world. Values offered through commitment to the original Christian faith might contribute substantially to the awakening of nations and eventually to peace between nations. The ethics of embrace might stimulate a new desire in peoples for self-preservation and for ultimate flourishing. Volf correctly observes that Christians are not vigorous enough in confronting the world powers and challenging them to rethink their politics of exclusion. Being vigorous means being prophetic, avoiding idleness and coerciveness, and living up to the challenge the Lord has set before us.

46. Volf, "21st Century Thoughts."

How should nations approach the problems of exclusion and embrace (forgiveness) in the process of reconciliation? In his Calvin College interview Volf takes South Africa as an example, claiming that many people who supported apartheid rebelled against the nation's need for forgiveness, against even the very idea of forgiveness. There was a mismatch between national needs and the needs of individuals, and we must not forget individuals, Volf reminds us.[47] First of all, general willingness must exist prior to any reconciliation. The key question seems to be, How can we begin this conversation? As I mentioned before, Volf initiated the process of forgiveness with his *will* to embrace. In the same interview, Volf again introduces the responsibility of religions in this regard. All faiths have an interest in forgiveness. Elements of generosity and compassion can be found in every religion. There are examples of reconciliation like the Bosnian Franciscans (Catholics) and Muslims following the atrocities of war in Bosnia. In the most adverse circumstances forgiveness does come as a surprise, observes Volf.[48]

Hans Küng rightly observes that there is no reconciliation between nations without reconciliation between religions. Though Volf reinterprets and only partially accepts this remark, from my investigation of his ethics of embrace between nations (see above) I conclude that he has no aversion to Küng's principle.

In the *Payton Lectures* again Volf speaks about the relation between religion and the state. First of all, he recognizes globalization as increasing interconnectivity and interdependence, and notes the very rapid pace of change. Religions are caught up in this reality, but when they coexist no single faith can integrate society as a whole. This leads to decoupling society from a specific religion (as in the 16th century Reformation). Connections between religion and the state are weakening in some countries, but in others they are becoming stronger—examples include Zionism in Sri Lanka, or the Christian Right in the USA—as national identity and faith identity become one. Volf asserts that we should have no part in this because it is a totally mistaken perspective. The main cause of religious violence is alignment with the state: religion is the tool of state power. Volf properly warns that the majority of conflicts around the world are caused by religious exclusivism or religious identity aligned with the state. In *Flourishing* Volf explains:

47. Volf, "Giving Forgiveness."
48. Ibid.

The main culprit is the entanglement of religions with political power, either when the original articulation was made or as it was later transmitted, received, and its motifs rearranged. That's what defenders and critics of religions fail to see when they trace religious violence back to the basic flaw of human nature or to exclusivism and irrationality. Why do world religions so easily get entangled with political power? Their adherents twist one constitutive feature of these religions: the claim that a particular religion is the true way of life. Instead of being content to bear witness to truth and thereby honor the responsibility of persons to embrace a way of life for themselves . . . the adherents of world religions use instruments of the state's power to subdue and compel detractors. In the process, they reconfigure the religion, foregrounding its more bellicose motives.[49]

In this context globalization is the friend of religion, because world religions are already globalized. Globalization offers the opportunity to religions to come back to themselves because they have a universalistic vision of the God of everybody. Even Islam's link to territory is severed and Muslims live in religiously pluralistic societies, says Volf. Globalization opens the space for faiths to be politically pluralistic and to be engaged. *Will we enter the space?* asks Volf.

Volf obviously sees globalizing processes and religions' recognition of the common good as key protectors from atrocities and wars. The Holocaust is a typical example of how violent and atrocious religion can be, and how it can lead to national disaster. We have many "holocausts" today because peoples and nations believe that preservation of their own religious-historical identity means annihilation of the other. Serbian soil must be pure, Croatian soil must be purged!—even if these nations live in historical, geographical and cultural proximity, as in the current Israeli-Palestinian or Russian-Ukranian crisis. Of course, sometimes the course of a national agenda depends on the current political leadership. Going back, in general sense, to the positive values of globalization and the common good might help some nations to rightly remember their own past and to overcome the temptation of exclusion and rejection with forgiveness and embrace.

Volf reminds us that we live in pluralistic settings, and so we need faiths that are friendly to pluralistic forms of government in which each faith is perceived as one voice in a larger argumentative conversation. A state or nation must see itself as impartial and neutral, not ideological. It

49. Volf, *Flourishing*, 186.

must understand its "neutrality" as impartiality. It must provide space for dialogue, in which the state must broker the relationship between the participants in a fair way that is not preferential. The ultimate loyalty is not to the state, but to your religion. Liberal democracies should support negotiation regarding the good life and individual flourishing. There is no ideal in this sense. The USA or India are examples but still pure ideals. Freedom of religion and impartiality of the state are the prerequisites for religious dialogue and for public engagement of religions with a purpose of shaping public space and public decisions.[50]

Well, Dr. Volf, how compatible is religious freedom with action against false teachings?[51] I am against laws that punish apostasy and blasphemy, argues Volf. Apostasy should not be criminalized. Freedom of religion is not just freedom to worship but freedom to be publicly present and to speak with a public voice. The general nature of laws should be upheld and even the worship of Satan should be allowed. Individuals have the right, within the limits of freedom and equality, to set the direction of their own lives.[52]

If I am hearing Volf properly, the state does not have the right to interfere with any personal religious expression, in spite of its role as a guarantor of peace and religious freedom. History is full of situations in which this role of the state became ambiguous and paradoxical. Volf points to the structure of *pluralistic democracy* as the *only* viable state model which will ensure the prosperity of nations and the flourishing of both religious and non-religious citizens. Is his system of proposed non-interference of the state based on historical values of exclusively Westernized forms of government? Certainly, but it is not without perennial value.

What is the role of faith in these pluralistic democracies today? Volf responds: We should sensitize religions and Christianity in non-Western areas to be friendly to democracy; on other hand, pluralistic democracy

---

50. Volf, interview by author, July 8, 2014.

51. This question is based on Cameron West's evaluation of Volf's *Allah*: "He is sometimes too cautious in arriving at seemingly obvious conclusions (such as, that laws forbidding apostasy and freedom of religion are incompatible) and also carefully selective in his scope. In one sense this is fair enough, as his project already spans four volumes it's unrealistic to expect such an ambitious task to be undertaken evenly and exhaustively. Yet for all its breadth and depth, richness and warmth there is something about this book that, even if not actually disappointing, nonetheless still fails to satisfy." (See West, "Review of Miroslav Volf's Allah.")

52. Volf, Interview by author, July 14, 2014.

should be reconceptualized.[53] Volf might have expanded more on this suggestion, but I am not aware of the source.

Dr. Volf, would you respond to the following key question: How feasible is the ethics of embrace for *nations* today? How can we approach the governments and what linguistic methods should be used in reconciliation processes? After all, isn't this the substratum of all your effort to bring religion into the public sphere? A *sense* of embrace, explains Volf, can be applied across individuals, communities and agencies. Embrace has different dynamics in the personal, communal and political spheres. A person is not an abstract—he or she is already situated in a certain context. Social entities, however, have different dynamics, religious communities too. Regarding nations, the question of representation becomes relevant: who speaks for whom? Processes are much more uncertain and unstable and much more contested. In politics we have official representation, and formal authority is present. Communities, however, live without real structure. Religion makes things even more difficult, or it can make a bridge, on the other side. *Anything that resonates with the vision ought to be strengthened.* Personal life also has contestations of its own, closes Volf.[54]

One thing is certain: if we wish to see some results from the ethics of embrace we have to take into consideration *different* levels of human existence and the different dynamics of personal, communal, religious or national identity. Volf does not discuss these dynamics in detail, but we can be assured that *reconciliation between nations must include elements of personal forgiveness, peace among religious communities and embrace between individuals.*

One more important note on reconciliation between nations: in his column "Victory of Peace" (1999) Volf offers a Christian interpretation of the conflict in Kosovo and the purpose of NATO's bombing of Kosovo and Serbia. Though rather one-sided, the reflection concludes with an important Christian ethical perspective on reconciliation processes:

> If the perpetrators matter to us, our victory over them will matter less than the *victory of peace between them.* The logic of conflict demands victory, and often some kind of victory is essential to stop violence. But though love rejoices over victims' liberation, it celebrates not so much perpetrators' defeat as the reconciliation

53. Ibid.
54. Ibid.

between perpetrators who have been delivered from the captivity to evil and victims who have been freed from oppression.[55]

In other words, the focus is not on justice but on love and peace. Love strives not towards revenge but creates space for ultimate forgiveness and reconciliation as the only way to curb never-ending enmity and violence. The only way to enter this space is to be willing to *embrace* the other and be embraced by the other in the transnational and transcultural common search for the common good of flourishing *life worth living*. Am I, as a Serbian '*chetnik*,' willing to embrace an Albanian, *a 'shiftar*,' who took away the holy land of Kosovo? The answer to this specific and particular question will determine how serious I am in pursuing universal peace between nations and religions and life worth living based on the ethics of embrace, and how indefatigable I am in "bearing" the cross of Christ.

Faith and Economy

Do we live on bread alone? Isn't success the driving force in today's global market? What happens when success conflicts with personal religious conviction? How do economic structures and faith influence each other?

I will never forget my first student days in the USA in the 1990s. It happened that both my wife and I needed a dentist. This is a fearsome reality for many in the USA, but even more so for international students without appropriate and sufficient health and dental insurance. Eventually one of our friends found a dentist for us, a Christian from our religious community in good and regular standing. When we entered the clinic there was no smile, no welcome, no friendly encouragement from the dentist?! We realized something was wrong and almost decided to leave. Complaining and grumbling about the bill we would not be able to cover, he made us sit and "enjoy" the procedure. It was quick and painful. My wife lost her tooth, which could have been fixed, because of the financial "constraints" of this dentist. As we left we just mumbled a "thank you," even for extraction. Maybe he had a bad day. We wanted to forget the incident as soon as possible, though we were grateful for the "service." Later, I asked myself many times: If a professed Christian is not willing to help another professed Christian of the same Christian community without always being rewarded financially, how promising is the future of the Christian world and this

---

55. Volf, "Victory of Peace," 685.

world in general? Thinking about the money-driven globalized market and Christian identity I can testify that the clash of values is evident. Knowing that we do not live on bread alone, we still fully endorse the laws and principles of the globalized market around us. If our religious conviction does not stimulate economic prosperity, we can suddenly make a shift in our religious attitudes and behavior—why not? Everything is legitimate that leads to prosperity, longevity and health (especially our own)! Isn't religion just a pragmatic instrument towards flourishing? Let us turn very briefly to Miroslav Volf's proposal of faith and economy relations.

In his lecture *Values that Shape the Market*[56] Volf discusses the relationship between religious values and the globalized market economy. First he makes a distinction between two sets of issues: the moral and religious convictions underpinning the market, and the moral and religious convictions that determine the goals of the market. Regarding the first set of issues, Volf reminds us of Max Weber's observation: the Puritans believed that economic prosperity is a sign of God's grace ("God and Gold").[57] This belief is not found only in Protestantism—Judaism has another version. Puritanism was also based on emerging capitalism, or at least made emerging capitalism possible. Weber concentrated on individuals, but Volf argues that Weber's thesis is being extended today to social relations. Social capital is the ability to work together for common purposes in groups and organizations. In Francis Fukujama's project[58] the wellbeing of nations is conditioned by a single characteristic, the level of *trust* inherent in the society. Religions and values act in conjunction with the market, concludes Volf.

Regarding the second set of issues (the purposes or goals of the market) religion seems to be important (for many) only if it stimulates economic growth. In what way is economic growth important? Is it the ultimate good? asks Volf. Capitalism has been seen as part of a larger narrative about the meaning of human life and history. The goals are increasing pleasure and decreasing pain. According to Adam Smith,[59] Volf notes, the necessities and conveniences of life are justifications for economic growth, and we have become pleasure-seeking "animals." *But a life spent pursuing pleasure is empty, Volf concludes, and therefore a culture based on this principle is empty too.* Faith should contribute to promotion of love, not pleasure. Does

56. Volf, "Values that Shape the Market."
57. Weber, *The Protestant Ethic and the Spirit of Capitalism.*
58. Fukujama, *Trust: The Social Virtues and Creation of Prosperity.*
59. Smith, *The Wealth of Nations.*

economic growth in fact serve human flourishing and the common good? This is the key question posed by Volf.[60]

In his lecture "World Faiths: Politics, Economics, and Competing Visions of Human Flourishing," part of the *Payton Lectures 2014*, Volf returns to the issue of globalization, which, he believes, is *luring* Christians to betray their original vision. [61] According to Weber, early capitalism borrowed from faith the primacy of transcendence goals: material wealth is a sign of God's favor; material wellbeing has primacy, and things of ordinary life, health, longevity, and pleasures are emphasized. *Faith is pulled into the vortex of economic globalization.* Globalization pressures faiths to give up their own most unique insights and concerns. In *Flourishing* Volf argues:

> . . . as for most people on all continents, capitalist globalization rouses ambivalent feelings: it is both full of rich possibilities and brimming with uncertainties and dangers. I've experienced this double-faced character of capitalist globalization both from the perspective of its dominant core states (the United States and Germany) and from the point of view of the smaller and more fragile nations (Croatia). Both of these settings have confirmed my conviction that we should neither simply celebrate capitalist globalization nor simply denounce it.[62]

The mother of all temptations is to serve the false gods and to believe and act as if human beings live by bread alone. World religions, therefore, become instruments of mundane struggles over bread, concludes Volf.[63]

What can we do to alleviate poverty in the world? What can faith do in order to teach people that we cannot live by bread alone? What kind of language can we use to present this idea to the rich and powerful? These were my questions to Dr. Volf.[64] The practice of the church, contends Volf, should be based on the example of people like Pope Francis. Metaphorically speaking, golden crosses should be removed and global solidarity promoted. According to Volf, churches have the infrastructure to distribute food and medicine, and in some parts of the world religious communities become indispensable in this project. Rowan Williams, one of the

60. Volf, "Values that Shape the Market."

61. Volf, "World Faiths."

62. Volf, *Flourishing,* 6.

63. Ibid., 22-23.

64. Volf, Interview by author, July 14, 2014.

inspirational figures in Volf's theology of economy, [65] in his *Faith in the Public Square*, teaches us that the tension between theology and economy should be resolved by endorsing a new theory, namely, "household theory." [66] Good housekeeping seeks *common* well-being and stability. This metaphor should teach us to use our intelligence how to "balance the needs" and "secure trust" in the economic climate of "maximized profit and unlimited material growth."[67] Simple as it is, the principle is derived both from the natural law theory and from an active principle of Christian compassion and care.

In the overall context of the relationship between faith and the economy Volf has also developed an extensive theology of human work, starting from a Marxist position and moving toward the value of work in the Spirit.[68] He explains:

> To state that neither work nor the product of work should be a mere means but should also be ends in themselves is to maintain that every good worker goes out of herself and loses herself in her work. Without such "self-forgetfulness," in which the inborn egoism that twists everything into means for our ends loosens its grip on us, there is no true joy in work. The opposition between the self-forgetfulness in work and self-realization through work is only apparent. Just as "everything else" will be added to us when we seek the Kingdom of God (Matt. 6:33), so will self-realization be added to us when we seek good work, when we serve others by self-forgetful enjoyable work that does not violate our personhood.[69]

After all, the purpose of work and economy is to promote human flourishing and the common good, not by the accumulation of wealth and pleasure but on the basis of the principle of love, service and embrace of the other. Work, in other words, has no inherent transcendent value and should not be deified; its value is instrumental, but its final purpose is not "the wealth of nations" but the promotion of life worth living.

---

65. Volf, Interview by author, July 14, 2014.

66. Williams, *Faith in the Public Squar*, 227.

67. Ibid.

68. Volf, *Work in the Spirit: Toward a Theology of Work* is a complete and detailed investigation of the meaning and spiritual understanding of work.

69. Ibid., 201.

This brief evaluation of Volf's theology of economy shows that his main purpose is to reemphasize the fact that humankind does not live on bread alone; for this reason a market, if it triumphs over all other forms of human relations, will ultimately deprive humanity of its purpose for living and of life worth living. Recognition of the contribution of faith and the transcendent vision in the economic sphere will eventually save the purpose of the economy itself and promote the common good. Volf's compelling vision for a faith-driven economy based on Christian values or general values of life worth living holds great promise of refreshment for the one-sided, self-destructive processes of globalization.

The Future of Theologians, Theology, and the Ethics of Embrace

The final word on Volf's theology and ethics should be, I believe, his emphasis on the roles of a theologian and of theology in the 21st century. Since theologians today are engaged in public testimony (perhaps unlike the post-Second World War era that was defined by the public engagement of philosophers, not theologians and ethicists), there is a need for this important contemplation.

Volf clarifies that 21st century theology is about changing the world. There are some of us, he claims, who are actively involved in this process. The goal of theology is God and God's relation to the world and our relation to God, and we have to speak about this reality, and its ultimate goal—eschatological joy. But we also speak about how this world should be now. There is no *status quo* since theology speaks to the world in the light of God's character. In that regard it does change the world. Theology, however, is not alone in this noble task. Politicians and economists are welcome to join. However, what if centers of world power and church power are not willing to hear about the change? Volf clearly replies that we should *testify* about goodness and truth, taking small steps and engaging in small "rebellions" of good against evil. This is hope. The symbol of this struggle was Abraham, who exercised faith and hope when God called, by packing up and leaving for the unknown land, explains Volf.[70] My modest contribution to the project is this work of a testimony about the struggle for reconciliation, peace and life worth living. My journey with Miroslav Volf has been transformed into a perpetual remembrance of both inability to perfectly

70. Volf, "21st Century Thoughts."

live up to the standards of following Christ in forgiveness and love, and willingness to open to God's miraculous power of Grace which embraces us and makes us 'witnesses of life worth living.'

The role of a theologian as a public figure, Volf continues, is to openly testify about the goodness of God, who has the ability and power to transform this world. Such a testimony offers *hope* to the nations and religions—*hope for embracing* each other in spite of our differences, hope based on God's wonderful embrace of us all. I admire Volf's insistence on *small* steps towards public promotion of transcendent divine values in this world full of meaninglessness, strife and turmoil. Courage to be and to act is what counts.

In my interview with him, I asked, What is the role of a theologian as a public figure today? Volf responded briefly but comprehensively: to take up the issues that move people and that are discussed in the wider society, issues that concern life worth living for individuals, communities, and ecosystems, and to address these issues from the perspective of a life sketched by basic Christian narratives and Christian convictions.[71] For Volf, this means searching for potential links between Christian theology and the varieties of human experiences, theories, and issues of relevance.[72] Since theology is a *way of life* and not just an intellectual construct it should not just play the role of critique but should make an attempt to construe and create a positive vision for human life.[73] Volf believes that the future of theology basically entails a call for the re-emergence of Christian integral humanism and for a critique of the kind of instrumental reason that ignores the vision of life worth living. We should strive to open new vistas of understanding of transcendence and encourage a new openness to the conceptualization of immanence.[74] Religious traditions and investigations of sacred Scriptures should serve the purpose of finding a viable way of life that is worth living. The great thinkers of the past should become the conversation partners of the present. They should help us to articulate today a renewed vision of transcendence that is relevant in the contemporary context.[75] This is exactly what Volf has been doing in his *Life Worth Living* project. In today's living of ordinary lives that seek for bread alone there

71. Volf, Interview by author, July 14, 2014.
72. Volf, "Systematic Theology."
73. Ibid.
74. Ibid.
75. Ibid.

is an obvious emptiness of meaning, without transcendent vision. In the immanent contemporary market-driven consumerist society Volf believes that the key element should be *contentment*. Christian faith in the future will have to articulate new ways of understanding the basic human need for satisfaction in the holistic sense.[76] Theology will then be transformed into an anthropological vision of life led well and life going well for the purpose of the common good.

Responding to a question about his vision for young Christian leaders today, Volf humbly admits that what he wishes for them he wishes for himself also.[77] First of all, it is the character of Christ, as the only genuine forerunner. How can we open ourselves up for Christ to live through us? Volf suggests that we need to make plausible the anthropological reality that to live with Christ today means to live the life of flourishing as opposed to the life of petty pleasures.[78] This is his final admonition for young Christian leaders who aspire to exhibit a living experience with Christ and to testify to it in fresh and innovative ways in the contemporary globalized public realm. I believe this is the main legacy of Miroslav Volf's work. It is also the goal of this modest project.

Thus, the articulation of a transcendent yet down-to-earth anthropological vision of life worth living, full of contentment, holy joy and relevancy, becomes the future task of Christian theology and theologians in this globalized world. Who is more content, joyful and relevant today and always than the one who is embraced by the transcendent and ultimate Other in order to willingly and joyfully embrace all others? Life worth living is an outcome of the enactment of the ethics of embrace.

76. Ibid.
77. Volf, Evangelical Alliance Interview.
78. Ibid.

EPILOGUE

I AM SITTING IN the Yale Divinity Library typing these last words of my Visiting Fellow Project. I am especially glad that Wipf & Stock accepted this work for publication. Looking through the window at an extraordinarily peaceful tree, I am daydreaming and contemplating the possibility of peace between individuals, religions, and nations in this world. Not a leaf is stirring. What a contrast to the turbulent world around us! ISIS, Ukraine, the new cold war, Syria, even Ferguson, Baltimore... Next week we have the International Day of Peace chapel at Yale Divinity School, and my now good friend Miroslav Volf unfortunately will not be able to offer the homily on this topic since the Center for Faith and Culture welcomes the presidents of two nations (Croatia and Macedonia) next week. What will be the topic of their conversations in these Christian academic halls? What is Volf's purpose in bringing so many influential public figures to the Center for Faith and Culture? What is, after all, the legacy of Volf's work?

He is a profound thinker who has done an extensive amount of research, a scholar who has developed some unique ideas about God, the Trinity, the church, and our daily relationship to others and the world. He is a fellow searcher for transcendence and light in this mundane and dark reality. He is an ethicist of embrace and a promoter of peace between individuals, religions and nations. He is a visionary of faith-friendly globalization and democracy-friendly religions. He is a Christian who has struggled to keep his identity within permeable boundaries as he negotiates the ecumenical quandary. He is a public theologian who has devoted his life to the promotion of the common good of religion in the public sphere. *He is a witness to life worth living*!

I am exceedingly glad that embraced and penitent "*ustasha*" and "*chetnik*" finally might receive hope in embracing each other. I remember my Croat "friend" in the trenches of the 1990s Balkan war praying and hoping that he enjoys life worth living, and I feel "I can breathe" now much easier . . .

BIBLIOGRAPHY

Armstrong, John H. "Bishop Tony Palmer and Pope Francis on Christian Unity." March 10, 2014. Blog at http://johnharmstrong.com/?p=6226.

Augustine, St. *The Confessions*. Translated and edited by Albert Cook Outler. Mineola, NY: Dover, 2002.

Baraheni. "The Mask of Your Limping Murderer." http://www.rezabaraheni.com/wp-content/uploads/2014/10/Two-Poems-New-York-Review-of-Books-10-28-1976.pdf.

Chambers, Oswald. *Disciples Indeed*. Fort Washington, PA: Christian Literature Crusade, 1960.

———. "The Unheeded Secret." http://utmost.org/the-unheeded-secret/.

Dávila, María Teresa. "The Gift We Bring: Engaging Miroslav Volf's Vision of Religions in the Public Square." *Political Theology* 14 no. 6, 2013: 758-71.

Fukujama, Fukuyama. *Trust: The Social Virtues and Creation of Prosperity*. New York: Free Press, 1996.

Heim, S. Mark. *Salvations: Truth and Difference in Religion*. Maryknoll: Orbis, 1995.

Hergenhahn, B. R. *An Introduction to the History of Psychology*. Boston: Cengage Learning, 2008.

James, William. *The Varieties of Religious Experience*. New York: The Modern Library, 2002.

Kierkegaard, Søren. http://www.goodreads.com/quotes/1005795-when-one-has-once-fully-entered-the-realm-of-love.

———. *The Sickness Unto Death*. 1849. http://izquotes.com/quote/243952.

———. *Works of Love*. Translated by Howard V. Hong and Edna H. Hong. Princeton: Princeton University Press, 1995.

Kronman, Anthony T. *Education's End: Why Our Colleges and Universities Have Given Up on the Meaning of Life*. New Haven: Yale University Press, 2007.

Le Pen, Marine. "Globalization is Barbarous, Multinationals Rule World." *Russia Today News*, rt.com, December 8, 2014. http://rt.com/news/212435-france-pen-globalization-barbarity.

Lewis, C.S. *Mere Christianity*. New York: Macmillan, 1952.

Li, Jessica, "Students and Administrators Discuss Mental Health Policy, *Yale Daily News*, Thursday, Dec. 4, 2014, 8.

Lituchy, Barry M. *Jasenovac and the Holocaust in Yugoslavia*. Jasenovac Research Institute, 2006.

Meacham, Jon. *Thomas Jefferson: The Art of Power*. New York: Random House, 2013.

Milazzo, Matteo J. *The Chetnik Movement and the Yugoslavian Resistance*. John Hopkins University Press, 1975.

Miles, Sara. *Take This Bread*. New York: Ballantine Books, 2007.

Mill, John Stuart. *Autobiography*. The Harvard Classics, vol. 25, Charles Eliot Norton, ed. New York: P.F Colier & Son Company, 1909.

Moseley, Alexander. "Philosophy of Love." *Internet Encyclopedia of Philosophy*. www.iep. utm.edu/love/.

Oppenheimer, Mark, "Embracing theology: Miroslav Volf spans conflicting worlds." *Christian Century* 120 no. 1, 11 Jan 2003: 18-23.

Ruether, Rosemary Radford. "Sexism and God-talk." In *Christian Social Teachings: A Reader in Christian Social Ethics From the Bible To the Present*, edited by George W. Forell, 298-307. Minneapolis, MN: Fortress Press, 2013.

Santic, Aleksa. "Vece na Skolju," 1904. http://www.aleksasantic.com/Santic/1904.html.

Santrac, Aleksandar. *A Comparison of John Calvin and Alvin Plantinga's Concept of Sensus Divinitatis: Phenomenology of the Sense of Divinity*. New York: Edwin Mellen Press, 2011.

———. "Untying the Knots of Thinking: Wittgenstein and the Role of Philosophy in Christian Faith." *In die Skriflig/In Luce Verbi*; Vol 49, No 1 (2015).

Shue, Henry. "Torture." In *Ethics: History, Theory, and Contemporary Issues*. Edited by Steven M. Cahn and Peter Markie, 903-913. New York: Oxford University Press, 2015.

Smith, Adam. *The Wealth of Nations*. New York: Bantam Classics, 2003.

Volf, Miroslav. *After Our Likeness: The Church as the Image of the Trinity*. Grand Rapids, MI: Eerdmans, 1998.

———. *Against the Tide: Love in a Time of Petty Dreams and Persisting Enmities*. Grand Rapids, MI: Eerdmans, 2010.

———. *Allah: A Christian Response*. New York: HarperOne, 2011.

———. "Allah and the Trinity: a Christian Response to Muslims." *Christian Century* 128 no. 5, March 8, 2011, pp. 20-24.

———. *Captive to the Word of God: Engaging the Scriptures for Contemporary Theological Reflection*. Grand Rapids, MI: Eerdmans, 2010.

———. "Conversations with Miroslav Volf, part 2." *Conrad Grebel Review* 18 no. 3, Fall 2000, pp. 83-102.

———. "Ecumenical Quandary." *Christian Century*, March 1, 2000, p. 248.

———. *The End of Memory: Remembering Rightly in a Violent World*. Grand Rapids, MI: Eerdmans, 2006.

———. *Exclusion and Embrace: A Theological Exploration of Identity, Otherness, and Reconciliation*. Nashville, TN: Abingdon Press, 1996.

———. *Flourishing: Why we Need Religion in a Globalized World*. New Haven, CT: Yale University Press, 2015.

———. *Free of Charge: Giving and Forgiving in a Culture Stripped of Grace*. Grand Rapids, MI: Zondervan, 2006.

———. "Miroslav Volf Replies." *Conrad Grebel Review* 18 no. 3, Fall 2000, pp. 63-66.

———. *A Public Faith: How Followers of Christ Should Serve the Common Good*. Grand Rapids, MI: Brazos Press, 2011.

———. "Victory of Peace." *Christian Century,* June 30-July 7, 1999, pp. 685.

———. *Work in the Spirit: Toward a Theology of Work.* Eugene, OR: Wipf and Stock Publishers, 2001. Previously published by Oxford University Press, 1991.

Lectures by Miroslav Volf

———. "Blessing or Curse: Faiths in a Global Order." Hong Kong University Faith Initiatives, 30 May 2013.

———. "Consider Forgiveness: Do you need justice in order to forgive?" 5 July 2012. https://www.youtube.com/watch?v=3fBzVkAF-tU&list=PL0BFF8D7195AE2F29&index=12.

———. "A Conversation with N.T. Wright, Miroslav Volf, and Mark Labbe." 2014 Payton Lectures. Fuller Theological Seminary, Pasadena, April 30 & May 1, 2014. Published June 6, 2014 at the site: https://www.youtube.com/watch?v=aNTz6QRVdg0.

———. "Do Muslims and Christians Believe in the Same God," Faith and Globalization, University of Fribourg, 2015, https://www.youtube.com/watch?v=dctS07Zqqo8.

———. "Life Worth Living: The Christian Faith and the Crisis of Humanities." Regis College Chancellor's Lecture, 22 Nov 2013, Regis College, Toronto. ww.youtube.com/watch?v=EVSCmlShIcI.

———. "Life Worth Living." Yale Divinity School, Youth Ministry Initiative Summer Study, July 23, 2013. https://www.youtube.com/watch?v=UpUxIynUA7Q.

———. "Multiple Faiths, Common World." Yale University, Feb 3, 2010. https://www.youtube.com/watch?v=HSw-VKmN6kU.

———. "Systematic Theology," Yale Divinity School, August 27, 2014.

———. "Values that Shape the Market." Yale University, 2009. https://www.youtube.com/watch?v=eT_1bBjRxRc

———. "Why forgive." The Veritas Forum, Brown University, 30 Nov 2010. https://www.youtube.com/watch?v=_SlAGFbj_ng

———. "World Faiths: Politics, Economics, and Competing Visions of Human Flourishing," Payton Lectures, 30 April – 4 May 2014, Pasadena. https://www.youtube.com/watch?v=XLuKpgWxxQE

———. "World Faiths: What They Are and Why They Matter." Payton Lectures, 30 April – 4 May 2014, Pasadena. https://www.youtube.com/watch?v=JnCJmBxSkbo.

Interviews

———. "21st Century Thoughts." Interview in Croatia. 30 April 2001 by Croatian State TV HRT. (HRT - TV Intervju:Misli 21.stoljeća - Dr. Miroslav Volf - 30.04.2001.) https://www.youtube.com/watch?v=t-LS2-Z7iSU.

———. "The Clumsy Embrace." Interview by Kevin D. Miller. *Christianity Today,* October 26, 1998, Vol. 42, Issue 12.

———. "Consider Forgiveness." Interview by Elijah Interfaith Institute, Sept 22, 2009. [Published July 5, 2012], https://www.youtube.com/watch?v=yBUsXIdHo4g.

———. Evangelical Alliance interview, Dec 10, 2010. www.youtube.com/watch?v=qMfOxdipEfo.

————. "Giving Forgiveness." Calvin College interview, April 5, 2012. https://www.youtube.com/watch?v=iTmX3Z4pDAY.

————. "Immersed in the Ordinary," Interview by Youth Ministry Initiative, Yale Divinity School, Aug 8, 2013.

————. Interview by B. Sarcevic, Religije i pluralno društvo (*Religions and Pluralistic Society*), June 2014, Sarajevo.

————. Interview by author. Yale Divinity School, July 8, 2014.

————. Interview by author, Yale Divinity School, July 14, 2014.

————. Interview by author, Yale Divinity School, July 24, 2014.

————. Letter, to author, May 2015.

————. "Public Faith" Interview, Baker Publishing Group, July 28, 2011. https://www.youtube.com/watch?v=FHqHSRD_y7A

Voltaire, "Tolerance." *The Philosophical Dictionary*, translated by H.I. Woolf. New York: Knopf, 1924.

West, Cameron. "Review of Miroslav Volf's Allah: A Christian Response." http://www.patheos.com/blogs/euangelion/2012/08/review-of-miroslav-volfs-allah-a-christian-response.

Wiesel, Elie. "Hope, Despair and Memory." http://www.nobelprize.org/nobel_prizes/peace/laureates/1986/wiesel-lecture.html.

Williams, Rowan. "Allah and the Trinity: a Christian response to Muslims," *Christian Century* 128/5 (March 8, 2011).

————. *Faith in the Public Square*. London: Bloomsbury Academic, 2012.

Wolterstorrf, Nicholas. *Journey Toward Justice: Personal Encounters in the Global South*. Grand Rapids, MI: Baker Academic, 2013.

————. "Miroslav Volf On Living One's Faith." *Political Theology* 14 no. 6, Dec 2013: 721-726.

Yeomans, Rory. *Visions of Annihilation: The Ustasha Regime and the Cultural Politics of Fascism 1941-1945*. Pittsburgh, PA: University of Pittsburgh Press, 2013.

Yoder, J. Howard. *The Politics of Jesus*. Grand Rapids, MI: Eerdmans, 1972.